Inspiring the Secondary Curriculum with Technology

Are other teachers using technology in their lessons? Are you letting your own students down by not harnessing the power of your students' technology knowledge in your lessons? Is your school asking you to show where you are developing ICT in your subject teaching?

Technology in your subject does not mean teaching databases, spreadsheets or word processing. Having *technical* knowledge is no longer sufficient, or indeed necessary, in today's world – more important is the knowledge of how to advise and teach students to use technology efficiently and responsibly through their subject. Students faced with a 'problem' will need to hunt the internet for open-source software, download apps and respond to the problem using technology as a problem-solving tool.

The scenarios are endless, but can be generated by the teacher – this could mean students publishing work through Amazon's Kindle or keeping a blog within a class wiki. Teachers do not need to have technical knowledge; rather, they need knowledge of trends and opportunities. They then need to blend their basic subject pedagogy within these new trends to contextualise ICT skills.

This book looks at pedagogical approaches to using technology in the classroom that will help you to harness future trends, technology and software and embed them into your subject teaching. Full of practical advice, it illustrates how secondary teachers – in any discipline – can accelerate their students' learning, progress and ability within their subject while developing the ICT skills needed in the workplace and society.

Including case studies and examples throughout, chapters cover:

- blended learning (mixing traditional teaching methods with e-learning)
- developing interactive students
- mobile technologies
- student safety online
- eportfolios and virtual learning environments

This timely new book will help you structure your teaching to harness the latest developments in technology in tandem with the students you teach.

James Shea is Senior Lecturer in Education and Secondary Phase Lead in Teacher Education at the University of Bedfordshire, UK.

Antony Stockford is Senior Lecturer in Education as well as running the secondary computer science programme at the University of Bedfordshire, UK.

Inspiring the Secondary Curriculum with Technology

Let the students do the work!

James Shea and Antony Stockford

LONDON AND NEW YORK

First published 2015
by Routledge
2 Park Square, Milton Park, Abingdon, Oxon OX14 4RN

and by Routledge
711 Third Avenue, New York, NY 10017

Routledge is an imprint of the Taylor & Francis Group, an informa business

© 2015 James Shea and Antony Stockford

The right of James Shea and Antony Stockford to be identified as authors of this work has been asserted by them in accordance with sections 77 and 78 of the Copyright, Designs and Patents Act 1988.

All rights reserved. No part of this book may be reprinted or reproduced or utilised in any form or by any electronic, mechanical, or other means, now known or hereafter invented, including photocopying and recording, or in any information storage or retrieval system, without permission in writing from the publishers.

Trademark notice: Product or corporate names may be trademarks or registered trademarks, and are used only for identification and explanation without intent to infringe.

British Library Cataloguing in Publication Data
A catalogue record for this book is available from the British Library

Library of Congress Cataloging in Publication Data
A catalog record for this title has been reguested.

ISBN: 978-0-415-84247-1 (hbk)
ISBN: 978-0-415-84248-8 (pbk)
ISBN: 978-1-315-74458-2 (ebk)

Typeset in Palatino
by Keystroke, Station Road, Codsall, Wolverhampton

Contents

	Preface	vii
1	Introduction	1
2	Blended learning	17
3	Mobile technologies and their impact on the secondary curriculum	31
4	Developing interactive students	43
5	Student safety	55
6	Eportfolios and virtual learning environments	71
7	The extended school	83
8	Embedding ICT in practice	93
9	Conclusion	105
	Index	109

Contents

	Preface	vii
1	Introduction	1
2	Blended learning	17
3	Mobile technologies and their impact on the secondary curriculum	31
4	Developing interactive students	43
5	Student safety	55
6	Eportfolios and virtual learning environments	71
7	The extended school	83
8	Embedding ICT in practice	93
9	Conclusion	105
	Index	109

Preface

Technology and software become out of date frequently – that is the nature of constant improvement and the desire of manufacturers to offer the consumer the next fad or development. The same can be said for any book trying to show a teacher how to use technology in her lessons. In addition, for a teacher, the ability to keep up to date with technology can be overwhelmed in the face of all the other things a teacher is required to do. Yet everyone is in agreement: if we could get our students to put the same focus and energy into our lessons in the classroom as they do their technology and screens outside school, then we would clearly be inspirational teachers.

In writing this book, then, we wanted to achieve three things. First, we wanted to take away from teachers the need to keep up to date constantly with new technology in ICT. The second was to show teachers how, without having to know the latest technology, they could get their students to focus on their lessons and learning with the same intensity that they reserve for their social networking, gaming and other technology. The last was to write a book that did not become out of date in a matter of months, but rather developed a pedagogy that could cope with the ever-changing nature of technology.

The end result has been a series of key pedagogies that delivers all those outcomes readily. The answer was through our central message: let the students do the work. In the same way that you construct your lessons through a structured blend of discovery and learning opportunities, rather than present yourself as the font of all knowledge, so the same goes for technology. Instead of presenting yourself as the person who knows all about technology, you construct opportunities for the students to transfer their own skills in technology to your subject.

There is some knowledge to be learned – understanding just what your students are doing when they are transfixed on their screens, but not necessarily which particular app or software they are using. However, the book does enable a teacher with very little knowledge of technology to be quite inspirational in how they harness technology and their students' knowledge of technology to deliver their subject.

CHAPTER

Introduction

Chapter summary

Inspiring your students
Modern technological students
ICT is no longer the preserve of the ICT department
Tablets and smartphones can do it
Ban them all!
Google it!
Software is constantly updating, why bother learning it?
You do not have to learn the technology or software yourself!
Example of a physical education teacher
Diversity of learners
Students can be inspired by technology
How diverse learners can benefit from technology
Key themes to consider: from behaviour for online learning to the online extended school
From technophile to technophobe
Explanation of some increasingly common terms

Inspiring your students

'Inspiring students' is a mantra for all teachers of all subjects. This is because we all know that, regardless of age, subject and environment, an inspired student will not only make rapid progress in terms of achievement and attainment, but they will also enjoy doing so. The other side of the argument is for the teacher – there is nothing better than teaching inspired students!

It is worth taking a few moments to consider what it means to be inspirational or to be inspired. Those that have been inspired report that they have been given permission to feel enormous passion for a subject. It has sometimes been described as *la grande permission* – that the teacher has created the environment in which a student discovers that a stream of dopamine and positive endorphins can be experienced through exploring and learning the skills and knowledge of a subject. The inspirational teacher works hard to create such an environment through a degree of personalisation – taking something that the student already likes and using this to refocus their perspective of the subject. These approaches can vary, but examples include English teachers getting their students to create Facebook profiles for Romeo and Juliet with online love messages replicating and using the language of Shakespeare through text and video. Or the physical education teacher who gets students to evaluate a song's beats per minute (bpm) in order to enhance the cadence of their running steps. Teachers are always personalising their teaching to their students in order to create this crossover perspective–where they converge the non-school life of the student with the content of the lesson–to show students that the lesson is not decontextualised content, but a genuine and valid part of their life. This contextualising approach to teaching is particularly suited to bringing in modern digital technology from the students' lives and using the skills and knowledge that they have already gained confidence in to help further their learning in school lessons.

Modern technological students

The student of today grows up with information and communication technology (ICT) at their fingertips. Their first book is just as likely to be on a tablet or ebook reader as it is on paper – one is not replacing the other; rather, the market has expanded to create the space for both. However, the experience of reading books now contains the potential to be more interactive. A child's first book may well be an interactive ebook that blurs the line between animation and text. As they get older, they might well read a book printed on paper, but still interact with the book through their post-reading experience. At the end of the ebook, the reader might *rate* the book, they might write a review of the book and they might share the fact that they have read the book and include a link to it – all through social networking with their peers. Thus another young person is increasingly likely to be inspired to read a book by a peer's online interaction with the book – although that book could just as well be on a tablet as on paper. One of the key things for a teacher to understand is that students are doing this in their undirected own time – they are doing this outside the structured learning experiences of school and, in the most part, the teacher will be unaware that the students are doing this type of collaborative learning activity online and in their own time. What we see is that students are using technology to interact with their experiences and that this interaction can inspire another student to engage with a learning activity. All a teacher has to do is to encourage their students to post their book reviews and links into one another's social networking streams and they have started to engage with using technology to inspire their students without having any knowledge of the technology whatsoever.

As a teacher, you need to make assumptions about your students – they are increasingly more likely to come to you with a range of skills and knowledge about technology. Your job is not to compete with them and to know more about technology than them. Your job is to understand how to take the knowledge and skill of an individual student and use this knowledge of the student to inspire them to engage with and love your subject as much as you do.

Using technology to inspire people has long been an easy option – you only have to look at a James Bond film or any Tom Cruise blockbuster to see how film uses technology as a suggestive and inspirational element of the story. That is not to say you can only inspire students with technology. The first story that anyone tells about educational technology is that the best lesson they ever saw was when the technology failed and the teacher had to be creative with their lesson on the spot. What they do not see is that it was the creative thinking that made the lesson inspirational – not the lack of technology. What technology does is harness itself to creative thinking and make outside-the-box, inspirational teaching even more possible.

ICT is no longer the preserve of the ICT department

Traditionally, teachers would point to the information communications and technology (ICT) department and say that the use of technology was the domain of the teachers in that department. However, many countries have changed their approach to this type of delivery of ICT. In January 2012, the Secretary of State for Education in England and Wales changed the landscape of how technology was to be taught and used in all state-funded schools. Out went endless lessons on PowerPoint and Excel and in came computer science. The ICT department overnight became the computer science department. In a way, this was not unexpected. Computing had been rapidly moving away from the notion of someone desk bound, using a non-mobile desktop to operate expensive software that was periodically sold and upgraded by the same company. The future, it seems, is in mobile computing – and it is moving into all the other classrooms and subjects.

Tablets and smartphones can do it

Teachers of all subjects have noticed the impact that mobile computing is having on their subject. Students are waving around smartphones that contain the power to perform a multitude of functions. But there is a large shift in notion – it is not the hardware that is being offered, it is the software. Instead of having a class set of dictionaries or calculators, the class already have apps for these on their smartphones. The smartphone can be an ebook reader, a GPS tracking device, a survey device – anything, in fact, that can be imagined, the smartphone can be. And if the app does not exist, the students can write a new one down in the computer science department to do the job. Why should a school spend large amounts of money replicating less interactive versions of resources that the students already own? It makes no sense – it would be better to have a policy that utilises these extant student resources and spend the money elsewhere.

Ban them all!

Some schools have attempted to stop this infusion of mobile technology. They have banned all electronic devices from the school – continuing to teach and run learning with a deficit of technology: interactive whiteboards are eschewed, wi-fi logins are refused, Kindles are frowned on and an artificial late-twentieth-century learning environment is imposed. Yet step into the world of work and we see the lorry driver running a traffic live SatNav on his phone, the mobile salesman running an entire office from an iPad, parents working from home or office seamlessly, online shoppers at Screwfix reading reviews of products written by fellow shoppers, the general public being alerted to supermarket sales promotions by apps on their smartphones and students being tracked 24/7 by their parents using tracking apps on their phones – society has upgraded, and some schools and teachers are struggling to cope with this upgrade.

If you think you are going to inspire students by preparing them for a world their parents have left behind then you have got the wrong mindset. That type of attitude to technology is not going to inspire students no matter how much you believe that technology is not always helpful. The students want to see that you understand the world in which they are going to work, the one their parents work in, the world they see on their TV screens. If you show them that you understand how technology is being used in your subject then they will have greater respect for you and there will be more likelihood that they will feel inspired by you. This is not to say that it is always right to use technology; obviously, it is not. Instead, it is for you to see that technology *can* be used in your subject and that you know *how* it can be used. This is the type of knowledge that is likely to inspire your students.

Lastly, the future is in wearable technology. Your students are going to be coming to school with watches, glasses and other forms of wearable technology. Are you going to ban your students from wearing their Pebble Watch? Even though it looks like a watch and contains a watch face, that watch face is actually just one of the e-ink apps available on the watch. When you are not looking, that watch is bluetoothing to their smartphone and transmitting information to that student. Instead of approaching the issue with a banning policy, you should be thinking about how the technology can help *you* to teach. Is it such an outlandish idea that you wear a Google glass-type device to help you access your own electronic long-term memory when you teach? Will the school receptionist send discreet messages to your Pebble Watch letting you know a student is late and on her way? *Embracing change rather than attempting to ban it will enable you to see how best you and your students can use modern ICT to help you to teach and them to learn.*

Google it!

If you ask a student a question outside school, for example when the Magna Carta was signed, what happens? They pull their phone out, Google it (if they have an iPhone they can just ask the phone orally, as Siri, iPhone's voice recognition technology, can do this) and give you the answer in seconds. You might say it takes time to do this or that they should learn this type of fact as part of their cultural capital. However, to the modern person, technology gives them the long-term knowledge they need temporarily and rapidly. Why bother to learn something that you carry around with you 24/7 in the form of a smartphone or tablet? Why not learn the bus timetable as well if that is your attitude?

If your student wants to know something, she will want that knowledge immediately. However, in the same way society has become disposable, so has knowledge. They can forget the date of the signing of the Magna Carta, knowing full well that if they need the information again at any point in the future they can simply request it from their smartphone (and in all likelihood by the time they need the information again the smartphone will have improved the speed, the quality of delivery and accuracy of the information being requested). At this point, you have to see how some knowledge and skills are rapidly becoming temporary. Google, and technology in general, is becoming an artificial aid to long-term memory to the point at which it is actually replacing some of the capacity in the brain for long-term retention of specific knowledge. In a world of constant change, investing time and energy in an inefficient way to recall something that you might never need again can be seen as a poor approach. Let us make that distinction again – knowledge or a skill that has a low likelihood of being needed again (or will have changed by the next occurrence) is fundamentally different from core knowledge or skills that are required on a regular basis.

Separating the two is the way forward – and ensuring your students know the difference between the two will be part of your teaching. We will write more about this issue, but do not see it as anything fundamentally new or innovative; society has been storing knowledge through the printing process for the last 600 years, and using modern technology is just the next natural step in this evolution.

Software is constantly updating, why bother learning it?

You spend all of that time learning Microsoft Word and then they change it to the new system. Which version of Microsoft Word are you on now? The 2000 edition? The 2007 edition? The 2012 edition? The 365 version? What if they brought out a new version each month? Would you bother learning each new edition each month? Or are you learning Microsoft Word in the same way we all do – when you need to do something you Google it, watch a YouTube video of how to do it and execute the piece of formatting you need to do for whichever edition is on the computer you are working on. Then, unless it is a piece of formatting you need to do regularly, you forget the knowledge as, by the time you need to do it again, the skill and knowledge will have changed when the edition is upgraded. This whole rigmarole is being played out every day by young people. The app they use for making changes to their picture is likely to be a different app next year. The app they are using will constantly update itself to a new version. The app they are using to network socially with their friends changes constantly. Each time, skills and knowledge are discarded and new ones assimilated. The mindset of the technological student is this: in the modern world (particularly around technology) skills and knowledge are learned and discarded constantly.

You do not have to learn the technology or software yourself!

This final point leads us to an overarching argument around the way we use technology in our lessons and the traditional arguments against doing so. Many teachers will say they have no time to learn the technology that they could use in their lessons. However, we are saying that you should not necessarily be learning about the latest technology for your lessons. Instead, you should introduce the notion of temporary skills and knowledge to the students. Thus, each time they explore a new area of topic within their subject, you should coach and train the students to ask: is there technology that exists right this moment that could make this learning or problem solving easier? The onus is not on you, the teacher – the onus is on the student to look at technology, explore the options and then justify bringing in technology to solve a problem or help expand learning or understanding in an area.

Example of a physical education teacher

A simple example would be a physical education teacher using complex maths with groups of sprinters and long-distance runners to put together running programmes that measure how lactic-acid-threshold training techniques increase speed and stamina. Traditionally, one would have to use stopwatches, clipboards, calculators and a large amount of estimation. Today, an app on their phone not only does all of the maths, but also takes the part of the teacher's oral instructions and frees them from having to run on a measured track as a system of counting and measuring their running. You might ask which running app does all this. And we would answer whichever one is the most popular and best suited for a particular type of runner or learner. At any one point, there is a range of running apps. Some are better for certain runners and certain learners than others. Students would select their own app as best suited them and then justify to their physical education teacher which app they had chosen and why it was the best one for them. The physical education teacher's job is not to train them in using a *specific* app, but to train them to select an *appropriate* app. This book is about adopting that mindset – letting the students do the work. Your job as a teacher is to direct and inspire them to use technology to help them learn and function even more effectively. Ask yourself whether you ever set a piece of homework in which you asked the students to evaluate which app on their phone would help them achieve their work in your lessons the best. Now consider how much work this requires on your part and how keen your students would be to spend the weekend hunched over their screens doing their best to improve their performance in your lessons. Here we see the philosophy of the book – let the students to the work while you are seen as the person who inspired them to do so.

Diversity of learners

At this point, however, we are seeing all students in the same mould, and it is patently clear that this is not the case. Students emanate from all strata of society, have different levels of disposable income and access to technology and are different in their abilities. However, a key theme among teachers is how to cater for the different learners in their classroom. The diversity of learners in the modern classroom is truly astounding. Since the movement towards inclusion, it is no longer a surprise to see the full range of society enjoying unfettered access to mainstream education. Visually impaired students with guide dogs are just as likely to be present in your lessons as students with severe autism – schools now make every effort to be as inclusive as possible.

The next step is to ensure that all these diverse students have an equal chance of success as part of the meritocracy of school. Where specific types of student do not make equal progress, then schools are charged with making interventions to bring about parity, and there are opportunities for technology to help schools achieve this aim. For example, there are some subgroups that have risen in terms of importance within the school – students such as the more able, students who have English as an additional language and students with special educational needs. Sometimes, these subgroups came about because of the subject involved. In physics, a lot of the work is focused on raising the number of girls who take the subject, whereas in English it is the gap in attainment between boys and girls that is the focus. It goes further than just the subject, however. Some schools find themselves with large numbers of students who come from a low-income background and this group is often targeted with additional resources, as in the UK, where they are labelled 'pupil premium' and schools are allocated an additional sum of money for each 'pupil premium' student they have. Any teacher or head of department charged with raising attainment or improving the progress in one of these groups would do well to consider the effect that inspiring these students through the use of technology will have. If there are funds available, it might well be that using technology as an intervention could bring a subgroup of students' attainment rates in line with that of their peers.

Students can be inspired by technology

Consider again what it means to inspire someone. Philosophically, it means to give someone permission to be subsumed by a topic or subject. When we talk about inspiration, we talk about students who are completely engrossed by the activity. The resulting experience is so intoxicating that the student seeks to recreate that experience by throwing herself into the topic or area repeatedly. At a simple level, an example would be a student who was not a good reader reading a book on a Kindle and thereby having a wholly different experience from that she has experienced earlier in her life. This might happen as the Kindle presents all books as the same to the external observer. It matters not whether it is *War and Peace* or *Where the Wild Things Are*, the Kindle does not present the book any differently to the *external* observer. This removes the stigma that many students have when they are publically holding a book in terms of the size, the length and the judgement external observers may make of the reader based on the book they are reading.

In addition, the reader can amend the font size to something more comfortable than the publisher's selected font size. Finally, the Kindle presents the text in small chunks at a time. The student is presented with the easily achieved portion of text to read, numbering perhaps 60 words at a time. Each time the student reads a portion of text and advances it, they get the feeling of movement and progression. All of these experiences can amalgamate and together can excite the student to read more rapaciously and regularly. Before they know it, their reading can double, triple and increase in such a quantity to the point where their reading starts to have an effect on their progress in a range of other subjects. The point of inspiration was quite small – perhaps a kindly librarian took the time to show a student how to operate a Kindle and then booked the Kindle out for them: many school libraries do indeed carry Kindles for the students to borrow. However, the effect of the inspiration was large – a widespread increase in attainment and achievement across a number of subjects. If we then start to think about some of the subgroups we were discussing, then this point of inspiration could have a strong effect on such a student. To elaborate on our example of the reader inspired by a Kindle, let us consider a young male student with a poor attainment profile who was a weak reader and from a disadvantaged background and who might not have access to books at home. At the same time, bringing books home might attract negative comments from siblings and parents/guardians. Inspired by using a Kindle, they might read copiously and begin rapidly to make progress in a range of areas while, at the same time, instead of being stigmatised by their peers for reading an 'easy' book, they would gain peer approval for owning a piece of technology.

How diverse learners can benefit from technology

Thus, when you are considering how to inspire your students with technology, you should think about the different types of learner in your classroom or playing field and whether the technology could help them as a subgroup or individual. Here are some examples that explore types of learner and how technology might be used immediately to help and inspire them:

- Students with spectrum disorder who can use a tablet to quickly transform texts into more suitable colours.
- Dyslexic students who needs to record themselves speaking and then transcribe their own writing.
- Students from disadvantaged backgrounds who do not have access to additional advice and learning opportunities in their home situation.
- More able students who already have the knowledge currently being presented through classroom materials and instead need to be able to research more extensive and challenging materials within the ordinary classroom setting.

The possibilities are seemingly endless, but it is important that you think about the different learners who are coming into your care and how technology could be the spark that inspires and ensures progress in them.

Key themes to consider: from behaviour for online learning to the online extended school

In this book we will revisit key themes repeatedly. Many of these themes are centred around bringing traditional concepts up to date. While more detail will be provided in later chapters, much of the concept of modernising traditional ideas is developed through the concept that teachers need to engage with the digital side of areas they already are specialist professionals in. As an easy and straightforward example, consider the area of bullying. Schools have been very switched on about bullying in schools for a considerable time. You will be aware, however, that bullying is now taking place online with the advent of cyberbullying. In Chapter 5, on student safety, we deal with this issue but, for the moment, consider what other traditional areas of teaching now also have a digital footprint and ones that you need to master. Thus, assessment for learning becomes assessment for *online* learning; behaviour for learning becomes behaviour for *online* learning; and the extended school becomes the extended school *online*. None of these replace the existing strategies, rather they take into account how these strategies have been affected by the way that all of this learning and interaction now takes place online, both in school systems and private social networking systems, and how the modern teacher needs to be just as good in the online equivalents as they are in the physical classroom versions. In the various chapters that follow, all of these concepts will be explored in detail so that you can be the teacher who can inspire students online as well as in the classroom.

From technophile to technophobe

It would be a mistake to assume either that all young people are extremely keen about technology or that all teachers are technophobic. The truth is the same for both demographics – there is a range of opinion from technophile to technophobe and you will be working with them all. However, as a teacher you have to overcome your natural aversions to some things as that is the nature of being a teacher. This is not always true for students, however. It may be that you are the one introducing them to new technologies in education for the first time and they might just not be as super-keen as you were expecting them to be!

For many learners, the biggest barrier to learning something new is 'fear'. Fear of the unknown and the fear of failure. As Franklin D. Roosevelt said in 1932: 'The only thing we have to fear is fear itself', so it is an accepted and effective practice for teachers to use familiar contexts and environments as vehicles via which new knowledge, skills and learning can be developed. By the same token, this same fear is the main barrier to teachers using a range of technology to enhance the teaching and learning environment. Occasionally, teachers feel that the students will know more about technology than they do and are uncomfortable being in a relationship in which they are the people with less knowledge.

However, it is our contention in this book that having current and in-vogue knowledge of ICT is not necessary to be an inspirational teacher. It is the job of the teacher to harness and utilise the knowledge that the students have rather than being the font of all knowledge in ICT. It is important, then, that teachers understand two core aspects concerning technology.

First, in terms of the hypothetical student who seems to know a lot about technology; when it comes to it, they will only really know a limited amount and, for the most part, this is wholly contextualised to their immediate experiences. What is modern and current to one student will be obsolete to another. The second core aspect is that ICT does not just mean computers. ICT refers to any media that enable or encourage communication – a fundamental notion for this book. Most of the ideas presented do not centre around using a computer as the main means of enhancing learning. If your previous attitude was that ICT is about computers and that you simply do not have the time to learn or arrange these resources then not only will this book help you, but it will reinforce for you that the second component of your belief is correct. You do *not* have time to learn or arrange these resources – you should be letting the students do all the work.

We hope you find the book useful and that it indeed inspires you to inspire your students. The book is designed to be accessible for any teacher, regardless of their knowledge of ICT (or lack of it). It is not designed to teach you a large amount of specific knowledge around technology; it is instead designed to teach you how to use technology to inspire your students – and there is a difference.

Explanation of some increasingly common terms

We would be remiss if we did not include some basic ICT terms at times and it may be you have not heard of some of the terms and want some immediate input to continue reading the chapter. While this book is aimed at regular teachers who would not identify themselves as either technophobe or technophile, it can be helpful to have some definitions in case you meet some terms in your work and simply cannot move forward without a straightforward explanation of some of them. However, we simply cannot cover every single term in ICT and so we do encourage you to copy your students and Google terms you are unsure about but, at the same time, wherever possible, we will try to give you a basic explanation of the most common terms.

This list is by no means exhaustive, mainly because specific ICT terms keep appearing almost daily and then tend to subside into obscurity again.

Android

Is an operating system for mobile devices in the same way that Windows Mobile from Microsoft is an operating system and iOS is Apple's system. The main provider for Android operating systems is Google. This class of operating system is aimed at mobile devices which, although they may 'talk' (communicate) with non-mobile devices such as a PC, do not have the same range of applications that a PC will have. Where they do offer this, it is likely to be cloud based (see cloud computing).

App

App is actually just a short form of 'application software' but, as most of the applications are aimed at mobile devices, the term is associated more with 'mobile application', 'mobile app' or just 'app'. A mobile application is application software designed to run on smartphones, tablet computers and other mobile devices. Some apps can be used on any mobile device, whereas some mobile device providers limit the apps that might be used. Often they will be popular ones and the provider charges the user a fee to download and install the app. More and more businesses are offering either a free app that can be downloaded to a mobile device, or place a QR code, which is a box with a pattern of squares on it. With a QR code reader on a mobile device we can be taken directly to the businesses website, which is a quick and efficient way of getting there.

BYOD

This means 'bring your own device'. It is also known as BYOT (i.e. bring your own technology). More specific variations on the term include bring your own computer (BYOC), bring your own laptop (BYOL) and bring your own PC (BYOPC). The opportunity here refers to students being able to use an ICT device of their own to enhance their learning. BYOD could be a mobile phone, a smartphone, a tablet, a laptop, a netbook, etc. It allows students to access virtual learning environments (VLE) remotely from outside the school as well as within a directed school environment. Many businesses are adopting a BYOD policy as people will pay considerably more for their own devices and will update them more frequently than a school IT budget will allow.

Cloud computing

This has tended to be shortened to the term 'cloud'. In the simplest terms, cloud computing means storing and accessing data and programs over the internet instead of on your own computer's hard drive. The cloud is just a metaphor for the internet. The main perceptual association of the cloud is that that you do not have to be connected to your computer to be able to access your files or programs. This is not strictly true, but comes about because people often refer to the cloud when using wireless devices such as tablet computers, smartphones, etc. You are able to store your files on the cloud and work on them from any computer that is connected to the internet, either by wi-fi or cable. The main feature of cloud computing is that a user can access a fully functioning suite of software applications in the same form as they have on their home computer. More and more software providers are not supplying a full program to put on your home computer, but provide one that looks as though it is a full program. However, many of its features are cloud based and you can only access them from your home computer.

Cloud storage

This is a part of the cloud system that offers a facility for people or organisations to store their data securely, which they are then able to access at a point, time and place suitable to their own needs. This is a really useful function to enhance student learning as we shall see later when illustrating some the different ways of using media. From an education standpoint there are, for our purposes, two forms of cloud storage: public cloud and private cloud. Put simply, public cloud is a storage network that any user can subscribe to or access for storing data, whereas the private cloud limits the access to specific users.

Looking first at the public cloud: there are a number of providers of public cloud storage, among the most well-known being Skydrive from Microsoft, Google Docs©, iCloud© and Amazon. You get access to Skydrive most easily when you buy Microsoft Office 2013. You are offered a useful level of cloud-based storage with the package and you access it by signing up to a Microsoft account (which at the time of writing is free). For Google Docs©, you sign up to Google Drive, for which they prefer you to open a 'gmail' account. This is just a Google-based email account. iCloud© is a basic level of storage offered by Apple, but if you wish to extend this Apple has a scale of charges. Amazon, which is part of the online company, offers a pay-as-you-use service. With public cloud, the service is offered to the general public on a free or pay-per-use basis.

Looking now at private cloud: here the service is managed by the organisation it serves and the access is limited accordingly. A school could use a public cloud, but could also operate a private cloud just for people directly involved with the school. This could be a particularly useful approach for a flipped classroom approach.

Drag and drop

This is where you can move a file from one place to another place. For example, you want to move some photos that you have taken from the camera's memory card to your computer. You could plug the camera into your computer and it will then transfer all the photos on that card to the folder that your camera has made on your computer, and then you try to find where it has put them (Sony creates a folder called 'Image Transfer' and puts them in there every time). If you only want one particular photo you can select it (click once on it) on the memory card and then either copy and paste it into your 'My Pictures' folder (if you are using Microsoft Windows) or select it, keeping the left-hand mouse button depressed and then drag it to your 'My Pictures' folder and release the mouse button. You will have moved the picture to where you want it to be located.

External memory

This refers to devices that enable you to save files (text, pictures, audio, video, etc.) and take them from one device and use them on another. For example, taking pictures from your camera and putting them on your computer. External memory comes in a number of forms, the most common being the following:

Flash drive

Also known as a USB memory stick, a flash drive is a portable data-storage device. They can store a whole range of file formats such as text files, graphics, spreadsheets, video, audio, music, etc.

Memory card

These tend to be used in audio-visual devices such as digital cameras, camcorders, mobile telephones (smart or otherwise) and tablet computers. They are referred to as SD cards, HD cards and microcards. Usually memory cards are available in large storage sizes so that they can store movie or digital film footage. Also, if you store a digital image (photo) in a high-resolution format (known as a '.tiff'), this uses a lot of memory. The size that you can use is usually limited by the device that you are planning to use with it – so check first.

External hard drive

These are more robust forms of mobile storage and can best be likened to having your computer's memory with you wherever you want. These are usually available in sizes similar to your desktop PC's hard drive so that you can carry everything you need to where you need it. These external hard drives are usually plug and play, but the large ones often need an external power supply.

Internet

The internet is a global system of computer networks (a network of networks) via which users at any one computer can, if it has permission, acquire information from any other computer. It was conceived in 1969 and is also referred to as the 'net'.

Plug and play

This is when you attach a device such as a memory stick, a mouse or a webcam (see Chapter 7) to your computer and it links it to your computer so that you can use it without having to add any programs to make it work.

Smartphone

A smartphone is a mobile phone, but it has more advanced features than a basic mobile phone such as a flat touch screen and the ability to load and delete temporary apps. They can perform all the functions of a basic mobile phone with the addition of such features as wi-fi, and third-party apps and accessories. They are likely to have access to more advanced communication technology such as 3G and 4G, which allow more effective streaming of video.

Streaming

This is where data are transferred over the internet in a continuous stream. Applications can display the data before the entire file has been transmitted. This can be seen with both music and YouTube files.

3G and 4G

3G and 4G refer to the speed at which a mobile device accesses the provider's network. Speed of internet on a phone or tablet is crucial to an app being able to function as powerfully as anything on a PC. In particular, more speed means that smartphones and tablets can be used for streaming video with ease.

Virtual computing

This is where a device is able to use software applications or storage facilities stored directly on another device (smartphone, tablet, PC, etc.). Typically, in a travel agency, the holiday consultant only has a screen and a keyboard and no actual computer. Although it looks as if they have all the holiday booking information in front of them, it is, in fact, all held on another computer, usually at a central data-processing centre miles away. So what you and the consultant see is a virtual display of the holiday booking and not the actual data. This is important so that all the consultants can access information, wherever they are based and in real time, which could not happen if there were an individual database for each travel consultant. Most schools have a virtual learning environment (VLE), in which teaching resources can be stored and accessed accordingly. Increasingly, in the modern office, a worker will access their VDT (virtual desktop) from any actual PC. The software and stored files will all be available through the VDT, regardless of where the user logs in from.

World wide web

This is *not* the internet. The world wide web, or 'web' for short, consists of pages that can be accessed by a piece of software called a web browser, and when you type a query term into your web browser a request is sent via the internet to look for pages that have data that match your query.

CHAPTER

2

Blended learning

Chapter summary

What is blended learning?
The flipped classroom
Using technology to deliver blended learning
Unsupervised learning can be increased
Beginning your blended-learning strategy
Reducing the workload
Learning can occur at any time
Encouraging collaboration within the blended learning
The learning community
Structuring online group work
Example of blended learning in history
Creating a relationship between online and classroom learning
Is your blended-learning strategy successful or not?
Using the cloud to run and organise blended learning

What is blended learning?

Blended learning is term used to refer to a teacher blending online learning opportunities with physical learning opportunities in the classroom or on the sports field. It is not dissimilar to setting homework to reinforce the learning going on in the lesson. However, in blended learning, the 'homework' is part of an online structured learning experience rather than a piece of work that is similar to that completed in the lesson time but undertaken independently of the classroom. Blended learning also blurs the concept of time; students can be working on your subject area at any point in time and thus the notion of fixed 'learning hours' in the way of timetabled lessons is eroded. The notion of blended learning has been around for some time, and it is beginning to have an impact on a range of teaching strategies. For example, there has been a shift in recent times to something called a 'flipped classroom', in which the teacher takes advantage of the way blended learning occurs to move activities for learning around on the timeline.

The flipped classroom

In simple terms, in a flipped classroom the learning takes place outside the formal teaching environment, and the critical reflection and assessment takes place in the physical lesson. The theory of the flipped classroom drew from ideas around 'flipped teaching', a form of blended learning in which students learn new information online by watching video lectures, usually at home, and what used to be the independent homework would now be done in class with teachers offering more personalised guidance and interaction with learners, instead of lecturing or using other information-giving strategies. The notion of flipped classrooms is explored in greater depth later on in this chapter.

Using technology to deliver blended learning

In the context of inspiring students and enhancing learning, we are taking a different approach to flipped classrooms. Instead, our philosophy of pedagogy recommends that you use active learning through a range of activities that incorporate ICT in an innovative way. For example, the learning activity may be constructed around a task that the students undertake outside the classroom or in extended learning zones around the school. It may not necessarily be an activity that results from teaching in the classroom; instead, the briefing may be delivered in the classroom and as a result the learners go beyond the classroom and undertake the activity. Thus the students then go the location or locations at which the learning is to take place and carry it out. Depending on the activity, they may upload their activity outcomes via the cloud before returning to the classroom where they assemble, analyse and evaluate their practice and learning. This does not, of course, mean that the students are ranging around the school unsupervised, rather it means that the structured learning activity, directed, semi-independent or independent, takes place in an environment outside the classroom. What you see here is that a broader definition of learning location can be adopted. Instead of there being 'in class' and 'out of class' we suggest these notions can be blurred to include more than one location and multiple points in time.

Unsupervised learning can be increased

What is happening here is that ICT is being used to provide a structure and information source in *replacement* of the teacher. This is not to say we are suggesting that ICT leads to removing the teacher; instead, ICT steps in, when the teacher is *not present*, to continue to provide a structure for the learning. Unstructured learning without a learned other will frequently struggle, but there is nothing stopping the inherent artificial intelligence contained within ICT from playing a limited but useful role in such learning situations. For example, a teacher might shift information transfer activities to the student's time at home in the form of a scheduled and structured series of interactive videos or reading and then have specific teacher-led activities within the classroom – such as discussion or other interactive methods in which it is important to have a strong learned other in the form of a teacher. Once you have grasped this concept, you can see that really it is just a question of shifting some of the activities around and taking advantage of some of the many online interactive materials available. Indeed, it may be that you have the students research knowledge outside the classroom and then evaluate and engage with the information found once back in your lesson.

Students are researching online information already and they are bringing this information into your subject area and your subject lesson time *independently* of your requesting them to do this. However, this research is usually quite unstructured and will vary considerably from student to student in terms of how much time, quantity found and the topic of the material viewed. A student might actually be struggling to research a topic very well and grow frustrated and demotivated as part of this experience. By your taking control of this external learning, and providing a better and more effective structure for the learning, you can reduce the weaker elements of this additional learning.

In addition to school-directed research, students will be reviewing online material and engaging with online learning simply because they are enjoying it as part of their personal life, and not because they are mandated to do it as part of organised and structured learning through their schooling. A student might be watching a music show on the television and interacting with the show through an app on their smartphone; they could see a cover of a song being performed and decide to access the original of the song being performed through their tablet – while the cover is still being performed on their television set! They might then, at the end of the song, post on their interactive feed for this show through their smartphone their commentary on how well the cover matched the original. This is quite normal multitasking and research-oriented personal online behaviour for a young person. An inspired teacher will see that behaviour and then realise that they need to gather more information about their students' personal learning habits through ICT and begin to show the students how they can be used within the classroom. It is a bit like the English teacher who finds that a student is secretly reading online gaming magazines or sports pages and uses this as a platform to link and build the student's wider reading habits with the reading that is part of their English lessons. So you too should be harnessing information about what your students already do in terms of independent work that is facilitated through their access to technology. If you can perceive this activity as something that can be harnessed for your own subject, then you are well on your way to inspiring your students to be thinking about your subject while they are undertaking their own personal online activities in their own time.

All of these skills that the students have developed in their personal time can be transferred across to your subject, and it is by drawing parallel lines across them both that you show students how to be more sophisticated in their approach to studying your subject.

Beginning your blended-learning strategy

At a basic level, the first thing to consider is what online learning opportunities you are going to offer as part of your blended-learning strategy. This will range from a low-key, online offering in which you direct students to commercially available resources to where you use the school's online area to offer students access to a range of activities when they are out of your lesson.

A poor model of a blended-learning strategy would be where a school uses the online area as a repository for files and instructions on homework. Who wants to log into an online area just to find out what the homework is? It is easy for the enterprising student to avoid the homework and say something along the lines of 'my internet was down', 'the logon did not work', 'my computer crashed', etc. Does that sound like an inspired student to you? Even further, if you already have a highly successful and functioning homework system, why are you making changes? If you switch to a new system then it ought to offer further and more effective learning opportunities. Nothing is worse than the 'high-tech' school or teacher adopting new technology for the sake of the technology with no new or enhanced learning offered. The first rule of measurement when you are thinking of using ICT to inspire your students is this: it must offer *an enhanced learning experience*. A school that places its homework online instead of issuing it in the lesson will point to the ease of access and the ability of parents to view the homework.

However, the students will have to go through the process of logging on simply to access the same homework they would have got in the lesson anyway. This means that the new model of homework, offering it *only* online, is inferior to the old model – offering it in the classroom with an ability to ask questions and check understanding. At this level of blended learning, a school should continue to issue the homework in lessons and, *in addition*, have the homework made available online for parents and absent students to access as they need or want to. This would then remove the inefficiency and also create additional learning opportunities for those who were absent or parents who are looking to help their child with their homework. Good pedagogy suggests that homework should be set early in the lesson so that students can ask clarification questions around it and also so they see how it links to the lesson involved. This example shows how you need to be thinking about blended learning: is it helpful? does it drive more learning? will it be welcomed? is it efficient? Is your school spending a fortune on tablets only to put the same worksheets they were using before onto the tablets? These questions will help you begin to see how to inspire your students with ICT. Teachers who use ICT to make their learning more efficient, i.e. *more learning in less work*, will always find students quite inspired by their offerings. Everyone likes the idea of less work and more learning!

Reducing the workload

There have been some complaints from teachers who have attempted to engage with blended learning. For example, some teachers complain that they do not have the time to 'put lots of things up' on the virtual learning environment (VLE). This tells you what they think the VLE is for – as a repository for documents and resources. However, if they did this they would be competing with every other professional online resource centre – and the truth is the online professional and commercial sites are going to be more efficient than the teacher. Why would you want to reinvent the wheel and write out an entire guide to Shakespeare's *Romeo and Juliet* when there are tens of hundreds of them online? The correct answer would be to ask the students to review an existing online guide to *Romeo and Juliet* and post it in the online area of the class with some sort of formative assessment and a link to the guide for students who want to see the original evidence themselves. The students could then self-select the best guides by reading one another's reviews and offering peer-to-peer assessment. Your job as a teacher should be to teach them how to select high-quality guides and to write interesting and detailed reviews as well as provide sensible and informative peer reviews. Thus, in a flipped classroom, a teacher might ask students to review a guide at home, but then once back in the lesson they would start to engage with what sort of criteria they were using and the skills sets needed to make a strong decision. They would then direct the students back online (in their own time) to start to engage with each other's reviews and offer contrasting opinions. What you rapidly experience here is that the inspirational teacher online is the same as the one in the classroom: tasks are student centred, involve research and critical writing skills and assessment for learning (AfL) has been built into the task. It is not such a big step to start to blend the two learning areas together. By undertaking tasks in the classroom – perhaps group discussion around what makes a good online guide – that feed into the online task, you are beginning to blend together the learning online with the learning in the classroom.

Learning can occur at any time

This example brings to the forefront a clear notion: that there has been a shift in modern society towards the notion that specific, school-contextualised learning can occur at any time through ICT. The education of students does not begin with their entering school and finish with them leaving the school premises; and that is something that has been embraced for a long time with the advent of homework to extend the learning beyond the school and into the home, thus encouraging students to develop autonomous learning skills. However, by utilising the online space in the school's VLE and the notions of the flipped classroom, a teacher can begin to blend the two together much more effectively. At the very least, you should be directing your students to undertake tasks using ICT outside the classroom which mirror what you would expect them to do as fully independent learners. This type of task requires no extra knowledge or online provision on your part, and the results can form part of the next lesson thus enshrining the best pedagogy in the use of homework: lessons that are built around the homework undertaken show and reinforce that the homework is valid and worthwhile.

Encouraging collaboration within the blended learning

The first major theme to embrace in developing your blended learning is collaboration between your students in their learning. New developments in international testing as part of the *Programme for the International Assessment for Adult Competencies* (PISA) have focused on testing for collaborative problem solving, seeing this as an indication of the kind of skills future adults will need in order to function in the workplace. The days of the lone worker who works in an office on their own are disappearing. The move towards open-plan office environments and online collaboration and communication as part of networked teams is the way in which modern office work is evolving. Teachers have an opportunity to develop this skill set by seeing their classes as learning communities rather than groups of individuals. Your class, as a community, is interacting through ICT *already* as part of social networking. Do not think it is not currently happening – it is. As a teacher, you need, first, to recognise that it is already happening in an unstructured way and, second, to start to put into place a structure to bring this interaction and learning to more members of your learning communities thus reinforcing one of the central themes of this book: behaviour for *online* learning.

The learning community

The notion of the learning community has thus been bolstered by the capacity of ICT to facilitate a community on a regular basis, and the inspirational teacher should be thinking about designing activities to enhance the notion of *the learning community*. The students need to start to identify and recognise that they are in a whole range of learning communities and that one of these communities is your particular class. You will already do this in some ways when you undertake group work in your classroom. As part of good behaviour-for-learning principles, you will probably instil good group-work habits, forming roles, rules and expectations of the group to ensure they function effectively. You might be teaching health and social care and, as part of group-work role play, have the students adopt personas and actions as part of this in your classroom, and it is this particular type of learning that you can use to start to consider how you can develop the blended-learning delivery that forms part of your teaching.

By developing group work *beyond* the classroom through online interaction, a teacher can begin to harness these extended learning opportunities. However, you cannot simply set group work and expect students to complete it online in the same way that you cannot set unprepared and unsupervised group work in the classroom. Just as you set out little role cards, placed an agenda and timings on the board and undertook a question and answer session on expectations *in* the classroom as part of your behaviour-for-learning strategy, so you have to do the same when you organise group work *outside* the classroom even if that 'outside' is actually at home and online.

Structuring online group work

The first thing to consider is developing differentiation in the online group work through roles. Some students will be better at research and bringing new knowledge to a group project; some students will have more artistic flair and be better able to organise the new information effectively; whereas some students will have natural leadership ability and be able to coordinate the group's efforts to a high standard to deliver a good-quality finished product. In particular, you should consider some of the learners in the classroom who, for various reasons, struggle to undertake the more challenging roles in physical class group work, but who might have a much better opportunity with online group work. For example, sensory-impaired students such as hearing-impaired and vision-impaired students might find that, instead of having to rely on the ability to hear and see things immediately in the lesson, they can use their ICT equipment at home or elsewhere to function much more effectively in the group work and take a leadership role that they might otherwise struggle with.

This line of thinking can run along all sorts of learning needs: the EAL student who has more time to frame and reference their answers, the elective mute who can at last express their views in a discussion, and the full gamut of students with specific needs, such as dyslexia, dysgraphia, dyspraxia, etc., all of whom might find that their performance in an online group activity is superior to their group work in the classroom. Now consider if that were you, if you were a student who had never had a chance to excel and then one day your teacher used blending learning to create an opportunity at which, instead of struggling and being a weaker member of the group, you found that you excelled, achieved and attained better than you did usually. Well, you would be inspired, wouldn't you? And that is what you are looking for with *your* teaching. You are trying to take good pedagogy of the type that you would usually use in the classroom, apply it to blended learning and then, through this strategy, inspire your students to be more confident, to like your subject more, to put more effort into learning and enjoying your subject and to make better progress than they would under a teacher who did not use blended learning.

Another consideration will be the type of artefact you would like the students to produce as part of the structured online group work, with an inherent learning *purpose* behind the artefact. For example, are the students trying to inform the reader or persuade the reader? Is the reader expected to interact? As a group, they need to resolve a problem that you have designed into the production of the artefact.

A group of art students might be challenged to produce a guide to modernism for younger students, and part of creating that artefact would mean a great deal of research and understanding of what younger students know and are expected to know. This can be applied to all subjects really quite easily – most knowledge can be represented in a range of artefacts for a range of audiences, ICT can be used to build these artefacts and, even further, ICT can enable a *group* to build these artefacts.

Example of blended learning in history

For example, a history teacher planning group work in the *classroom* might decide, as part of learning about World War II, that the students should engage with a wartime poster as part of a history lesson. They might decide to give different groups different tasks on the same theme. For example, one group could produce their own wartime poster, another group would have to create a drama representation and yet another group might have to write a patriotic newspaper article on the effects of 'the Blitz' in response to the poster. Yet, all of these things can be worked on both in the classroom and at home as part of a blended-learning strategy. The poster group could have a section on the project area of the VLE where they upload example posters they have found online along with comments on features and text they want the group to include in their poster. The drama group could upload a video of their rehearsal performance in the classroom and then upload links to clips from newsreels of the era. Again, the interactive notion comes in with the ability of students to comment as a group and draw on what they have found in terms of forms and conventions of such a scenario. Whereas one student in the group might be weaker at researching such clips, they are able to view the clips found by other members of the groups and offer their commentary – thus fully participating in the group work. The final group working on the patriotic newspaper could actually edit online collectively – each student reshaping and adding content and commentary as part of a Google Docs© file with shared ownership of the document. The connection would be in terms of having a physical lesson bookend this period of learning. Thus, the students begin their learning in the classroom, then collaborate online and then in the next lesson you might have a presentation and discussion on the poster, the Blitz article and the drama piece with discussion to follow it. The stage would be set then for the teacher to draw learning across the whole range of tasks together in a sophisticated contextualising approach so that the students understand the bigger picture of what they are studying.

Creating a relationship between online and classroom learning

This notion of creating and shaping the online shared area and how it relates to the lesson content is important. You can frame and shape the classroom-based learning to reflect what is going on in the online project space. In the classroom, you might introduce students to real-life resources from your subject that they cannot meet or touch outside the classroom, and you can then have them interact through structured discussion to frame their ideas and to challenge the ideas of others. There will be sections of your lessons where you are teaching content knowledge, but then that content knowledge enables the student to tackle the research task online with more accuracy and to understand what it is they are looking at and reading with better comprehension.

When you sit down and plan a scheme of work, you will often draw headings: lesson number, main activities, homework, resources, etc. However, a teacher who is keen to develop blended learning in their lessons will add a new section to their scheme of work template – which will be online learning activities or opportunities. Thus, if we think about the example from the example history lesson earlier, the teacher more traditionally might have set the homework for the students to be a role play of a diary entry for a teenager during World War II. However, traditionally, the teacher would probably simply collect them in and mark them with perhaps a few light comments of formative feedback. A stronger teacher might use them as part of the next lesson, getting the students to read a few of one another's examples. However, a teacher who was using blended learning might create an online area in which the students would be able to access real-life examples of war diaries from teenagers as well as upload their own. Weaker students would be able to review not just the real-life examples, but also the examples of their peers who had already uploaded their homework. Thus, those who completed their homework *first* immediately begin to enhance the learning of their peers who, instead of having to wait until the next physical lesson for the learning to continue, can continue to learn as part of the interactive homework that has been set. Students who were looking at examples of diaries from real-life wartime teenagers could then also link other examples they had found as part of their homework thus starting to take the workload away from the teacher and transfer this to the students. The next time the teacher undertakes this learning activity, they simply copy the links the students have found alongside their own to present an even stronger set of resources to their class.

In addition, following good assessment for learning *online* principles, they can quickly evaluate how much the class is learning through the online work without having to spend an enormous amount of time physically locating each entry in a physical exercise book, annotating the example and then returning the book to the student – all just to assess how well the students had learned about what it was like to be a teenager in World War II. Instead, this teacher can evaluate the online entries and then make modifications to the next lesson to clarify mistaken notions and fill in gaps of understanding. And the teacher can do this before the students have entered the classroom for their next lesson. There is no need to wait to see the class, collect the books, assess the books, return the books and only then adjust the lesson. Time spent on collecting, assessing and annotating paper exercise books can be cut down and faster, more immediate feedback online can be increased, thus maintaining the workload of the teacher, but increasing the impact of the formative feedback being provided. The whole process is quicker, more efficient and shows the students

TABLE 2.1 Example scheme of work extract with blended learning

Lesson	Main activities	Homework	Resources	Online activities
1	Explore war poster Watch clip of newsreel from World War II Establish groups and allocate roles	Write first-person diary account of teenager from World War II	War poster News clips	Diary entries to be uploaded to topic page marked 'Diaries' where real-life examples are also linked and modelled More able students asked to link further examples that they have found in their research

that their work is having an effect on helping the teacher personalise the lesson just for them. This notion of bringing blended learning into the planning aspect is important, and Table 2.1 demonstrates how a history teacher might lay out the plan.

Is your blended-learning strategy successful or not?

The easiest way to see if your blended-learning approach is successful is to look at the amount of traffic you are getting from the students. If the students are not logging in, interacting and driving their own learning then your blended-learning strategies have something wrong with them. The easiest way to discover why this is will be to conduct a whole-class or small focus-group interview. Ask the students why they have not been going online and undertaking some of the learning opportunities that you have offered on the project space. Sometimes the problem is not you – they might say that they struggle to get into the system, their passwords might not be recognised or they might not be enrolled in the correct place. All of these administrative issues might mean that the school's VLE administrative team need to look at the login issues or to organise whole-school training for the students. If your students have a technical issue then it is likely that all students have a similar issue and thus this is a whole-school issue rather than something for you to resolve.

Technology is fallible and sometimes it is the user friendliness of the system that leads to its success. If it is easy to log in and edit then a student is going to be more inclined to do this than if the software is clunky and frequently goes wrong. One easy way to check this is to have a fake student account that you use to check what it is like to be a student in your class. You can then see exactly what one of your students sees and encounter the same problems that your students encounter and thus be better placed to represent their issues to the school's ICT administrative team.

Traffic to your project area is not sufficient evidence of inspired learning – what the students do once they get to your project area is just as important. Your job, as a teacher, is to be able to accurately assess what the learning impact on a student is when they undertake an activity. Thus, tracking – just as you do in your mark book or spreadsheet – is important. When you set and assess work for the students in your physical lessons, you collect it in periodically, assess it and issue regular summative and formative feedback to ensure the students are making good progress. If you are offering opportunities for the students to work online or collaboratively, then you need to consider the same premise. Are you monitoring the evidence of online activity, grading it using qualitative and quantitative criteria and then checking the data generated to ensure regular progression is occurring across all identifiable groups? If not, how do you know that learning is occurring or that your blended-learning strategy is successful? All of this is important if you are to practise good assessment for *online* learning.

There is an additional reason that you should be undertaking online assessment: different types of student respond differently to different learning methods. Consider those students we said might perform more effectively in an online group activity as opposed to a physical classroom-based group activity. It might well be that you will find differences in attainment and achievement among those students with their online work. It does not have to be a student who has any particular identified need. Consider the notion that some students hate to speak in class; they will not raise their hands in debates and prefer to sit there not engaging with the question and answer session. When chosen through some sort of random name generator, like lollipop sticks, they are still reticent and awkward: it is clearly not their preferred learning style. Yet this same student might be the top student online in an online discussion forum. A science teacher might create a discussion forum around one of science's 'big ideas' – evolution or space and matter – and encourage the students to discuss their ideas in order to assess their misconceptions. The usually reticent student might thrive in such an online discussion, using their time to check resources carefully and to give much more measured answers with much more confidence that they would in the classroom. Instead of having to have oral confidence, they can utilise their written confidence and ability to research. Thus, we see that now they are no longer losing learning opportunities from non-participation in class discussion; this same student could easily transcend their natural standard and become far stronger – leading, ultimately, to a more confident and participatory student in the physical classroom discussion. In other words, the online discussion forum with their peers could inspire them to participate in the real classroom discussion – and from there start to enjoy the full range of learning opportunities within science and so forth.

Using the cloud to run and organise blended learning

We have seen from the explanation of terms that the cloud is a virtual storage and working environment. There are two key aspects of this. First, the cloud can provide a dynamic and real-time teaching and learning environment and, second, it can be accessed from almost anywhere. If you are used to saving work on a physical device such as a desktop hard drive or on some form of media storage device, you will know that you can only access these data when you have physical access to this storage device. Naturally, for the modern mobile teacher or student, this is going to be inefficient and prone to damage, loss and general inconvenience. The days of students bringing their memory sticks to the classroom are gone. Instead, the students will place documents on their online storage areas. They also can give access to an external person to this file type. This is not something that the school has to provide, this is something that the students are arriving armed with. Although more discussion about this will be found in the section on 'Bring your own technology', at this point you can assume that the majority of your students will have access to an online storage area. It might be that for disadvantaged students you make arrangements with your school for specific students to have access to training and provision of such resources as part of your strategy for having a school-wide approach to ICT that does not exclude or create divisions between students. This concept of students having storage areas in the cloud is essential to any delivery of teaching through blended learning. We talk more about the way students will manage their work in Chapter 6 on eportfolios and VLEs, but you will need to re-examine the concept that you as a teacher are the custodian and gatekeeper of all of the students' physical work. Why should a senior manager need to physically call for a sample of your books for a work-scrutiny activity? In schools and colleges with strong online resource management of students' work, this work is accessed automatically through electronic means. Quality assurance is thus much stronger due to the level of transparency when specific people can access any specific student's work at any time. This could include an external examiner who can simply access students' work on a regular basis as part of moderation and quality assurance through online access.

From a teaching point of view, the cloud enables a teacher to publish and share resources that either the student or teacher can edit in real time through online access. For example, at a simple level, one of the current methods of sharing a resource is through Google Docs©. This simply means that the owner of an online drive can grant shared access to a file or folder on their shared drive. Different permissions can be applied to the access rights. You can have any number of people who have access, but that level of access may vary. Two people, say the teacher and student, might have editing rights; while two further people, say the form tutor and head of department, might have viewing rights. Thus a teacher might publish a resource and an exam paper. The student might have only viewing rights to the resource, but editing rights to the exam paper. Additionally, the student might reshape the resources provided and create new resources drawing on learning within your subject. Being able to see original resources alongside the new reshaped resources enable teachers to better assess how much learning the student has undertaken and remove issues around authenticity and plagiarism. From the storage point of view, having an online area in the cloud allows learners to save their work in progress, projects, text, video, audio, etc., in a secure storage area and to access it from wherever they are.

What all of this means is that even if your school has no ICT capacity, no VLE, no online area, no provision whatsoever, it does not stop you from harnessing the facilities that students already have to deliver blended learning and thus ensure that your students are inspired to make better achievement and attainment in their time with you as a teacher. Take their current habits and simply start to use them to shape the kind of work you ask them to do as a group and in their own time.

Name: Aidan Turner
School: St Thomas More Academy
Age phase: 11–18
Your role: Head of Psychology.
Types of technology: It's Learning VLE.

Why you/the school introduced it: I wanted to increase the amount of independent work that the students undertook as part of their learning so that they moved away from the idea that all their learning took place in the classroom. In addition, I was looking to increase the level of self- and peer-reflection on learning so that the students understood that KS5 is much more about being a reflective learner who works within a group of students.

What was introduced and how?: It's Learning is the VLE that the school has bought into. I set up some project spaces online which duplicated what we were learning in the classroom. I then directed the students to these spaces as part of the lessons as places where they could start to place and engage with their research outside the classroom.

What problems or successes did you meet?: Not all departments use the VLE, so the students found they had to upgrade their knowledge of how to log in and generally post things. In addition, some of the students found it hard to make the transition from GCSE to A level and the increase in independent work. The more conscientious students were more successful in their online work than some of the other students.

What are the next steps?: I need to start adapting my written schemes of work to better join up the way I create online spaces for the students to undertake tasks online. Having students who have done it before means that I will have modelling to show the new students next year, and this will make things much easier once the students can see what previous students have done.

CHAPTER

3

Mobile technologies and their impact on the secondary curriculum

Chapter summary

The arrival of mobile technologies
A comparison between higher and further education and schools
Kindle – a device to help students read
Auditing the students and informing the parents
Convergence in mobile technologies
Reinventing the wheel
Mobile technology affects the curriculum and your status as the teacher
Should students really use mobile devices to learn?
Expansion of the curriculum
Personalisation of the curriculum

The arrival of mobile technologies

It will not have escaped your notice that mobile technologies have become mainstream. While early tablet computers, mobile phones and ebook readers have been around for at least ten years, it is the advent of three specific market-changing mobile devices of those types that have fuelled mobile technology use through to what is known as *the tipping point*. That is where take-up and market saturation reaches the point where the technology becomes mainstream and normal rather than being something for niche users or early adopters. These three devices are the iPhone, the iPad and the Kindle. Each has changed the market considerably – although the Kindle now exists as an app on both smartphones and tablets as well as being an ebook reader in its own right.

What was different about these three products is that they were immediately inspirational. Part of this came from the expectation built into people from using their traditional candybar or clamshell mobile phone. They picked up their phone – which was always switched on – they pushed buttons to either text someone or call, and then they locked it, still switched on, again. If a new text message came through they would pick their phone up, unlock it, read the message and relock their phone. The speed of the process could be measured in seconds. However, with the PC and email the process was different. The PC would have to be turned on – a process that could take several minutes at best. The email program would be loaded up and signed in and finally checked for new messages. If there were no messages, the PC would either be shut down or left in a standby or hibernate state – an expensive, energy-costly process. When emails became available on phones, people rapidly found that they saved an enormous amount of time. Thus, those used to text messaging quickly moved to adopt the notion of emails through mobile phones – and this extra usage meant that phones needed qwerty keyboards – the BlackBerry – or larger flatscreens – the Samsung.

The new Apple iPhones bundled with a virtual qwerty keyboard were an immediate hit as they enabled users to operate their emails and texts and access a range of information through the use of apps as well as the internet. This last point is the biggest point to consider from an educational perspective. Traditionally, one would access information through the internet. You would launch a browser, access an internet search engine such as Google and then pull up multiple providers of the same information – for example cinema times or an encyclopedia entry. With the apps that are found on smartphones (and now tablets and PCs), you would install the program of one provider which would provide you with this information. For example, you would download a single weather app which would locate you and constantly update your phone with the current weather. However, if you chose the wrong app, or an inferior app, the quality of your information could be weaker or of a poorer standard than that of another. Apps for weather have to take their information from a main source. The BBC weather app can draw from the vast meteorological information available from the BBC's weather team. An inferior app might simply draw information from a cheaper and inferior competitor. This means that the knowledge that the BBC's weather app draws higher quality data is important. In addition, as it is a market, the leading app may be superseded by a competitor and you could find that you want to delete an old app and replace it with one from its competitors. The BBC weather app might no longer be the best app and another app could supersede it. Indeed, one app might have inferior information, but be easier to use. This app could certainly be more popular and push another app out of the market. This is the point at which you, as a teacher, are starting to intervene. Your knowledge of the 'best' app is, at best, an opinion and, at worst, likely to be rapidly obsolete. There is little worth in establishing yourself as the font of knowledge on which is the best app.

As we will repeatedly make clear as a recurring theme for this book, your job is to teach the students the evaluation skills with which to choose the best technology or software – in this case, apps. Why, you will ask your students, is this app the best one for information? And then you will get them to rate how well it enables them to access or extract the information. This is another side of your teaching – getting your students to develop the skills they need outside the classroom through engaging with them in your subject. And at the same time they are ensuring that they extract maximum learning from their interactions as part of your teaching.

Returning to our timeline then, the iPhone and iPad ignited the market for smartphones and tablets leading its competitors to adopt the Google Android operating system in their efforts to successfully compete. This ensured that tablets and smartphones with apps were accessible at all price points. This further means that there is an increased likelihood that your students will have access to smartphones and tablets, but the range of apps and app markets they are tapping into may well be quite different. Frequently, you might make the charge that many young people do not have access to technology and while this charge is quite true, and we will discuss this issue in Chapter 7, you only have to look at any group of young people in any social gathering situation to see the true extent to which smartphones and tablets have become part of their life. Tablets, smartphones and other means for interacting with technology software or other people are here already, and it is the innovative teacher who grasps that point who will be able to inspire their students. Banning the technology or seeking to control it rigidly will simply prevent you from engaging with the young learners in a way that can help make them safer online and enhance their learning.

One of the key points of development occurred when Apple launched a tablet called the iPad. Tablets are nothing new, but they had remained a small proportion of the market until Apple launched its iPad in 2010. Traditionally, tablets mimicked a PC and would require the same starting up and shutting down processes. The iPad, however, mimicked the iPhone. Now, people could click the tablet on and off and leave it running in the same way they did their phones. This meant that the iPad became a very efficient mobile tool. Whenever you had a few spare minutes, you could bring your iPad out, make notes, multitask with email and research and put it away again. Indeed, Apple realised that there was space in the market for even more portability and thus brought out the iPad mini – designed to be more pocket sized and still with the capacity to enable the user to work from a mobile location at immediate notice. Competitors immediately brought out their own version of the smaller tablets, and we now have a complete range of tablets and smartphones of different sizes, all competing within the field of mobile technology.

A comparison between higher and further education and schools

At certain levels of education, these devices are becoming endemic. In lecture theatres and seminar rooms within higher and further education, many students will have these devices within the theatre or classroom. Lecturers and professors utilise this by pre-releasing lecture slide shows with embedded links *specifically for the tablet user*. Each year, bring your own technology (BYOT) enthusiasts within educational institutions are communicating with parents and students to suggest how technology purchases can further help the education of students during their time in college or university. Instead of letting students and parents guess which technology would be helpful, the lecturers are taking control of the situation and setting out the most efficient way that students and parents can enhance their education and reinforcing safe online practice at the same time. They are setting the agenda proactively rather than being passive and non-interventional.

Within many schools, however, there is a different story: tablets and smartphones are routinely banned; wi-fi systems are locked down and made unavailable to students; and teachers are banned from devising lessons or activities that draw on students' ownership of mobile technology. This is not true for all schools, however, and some innovative schools have embraced the smartphone and technological evolution and are creating learning opportunities for their students. However, at a really basic fundamental level, you are unable to do even the most rudimentary of interactive learning activities unless students have access to technology. This presents a problem for schools. Traditionally, they have invested large amounts of money in ICT rooms in which desktop computers were maintained with regularly updated software and hardware. Contracts were entered into in which outside providers would update the desktops every three years and the latest Microsoft Office would be purchased, installed and then taught by ICT teachers. Yet this purchase policy is both expensive and increasingly inefficient. The rate of obsolescence and updating technology means that the school will find it increasingly expensive and inefficient to keep up this policy. A school buying vast amounts of expensive technology and then updating it every year is unrealistic and a waste of finances – many of the students already have this technology at home and are updating their own technology on a regular basis. Some students need access to powerful desktops and subject-specific computers as part of their learning in a subject. Other students do not need the technology to be provided at all. If a student already has a laptop or desktop for their work at home, is it really necessary for the school to provide this technology again? (Especially if finances dictate that the school's technology is inferior to that which the student has at home.) Mobile technology, by way of contrast, has rapidly started to replace whole-school approaches to the purchasing of technology. By reducing their purchasing of desktops and diverting these funds into mobile technologies that the students own and keep as their own devices, schools are making the switch at a zero extra net cost. At the same time, it enables schools to find a way through the problem of some students having access to interactive online learning through tablets or smartphones when other students do not. At the same time, all students having the same *device* but being able to personalise the device with a range of appropriate temporary apps resolves the software issues and makes the device far more personalised to the needs of the specific learner.

As a teacher, tapping into this way of thinking means you should consider pressurising for a whole-school approach to the availability of and access to mobile technology. Encourage your school to network with other schools that have successfully made the switch to buying all students a mobile device and to evaluate how they create the financial package so that there is no increase in funding required.

Kindle – a device to help students read

The last device, which we mentioned at the start, is the Amazon Kindle. While there have been, and indeed still are, other ebook readers, it is the Kindle that reshaped the market and brought the ebook reader into the mainstream. And we do mean the original ebook reader itself and not Amazon tablets such as the Amazon Kindle Fire HD. This device was designed to make access to book buying a much smoother process. At the heart of its concept is the idea that you can pull up any book out of copyright, for free. You can also buy any book on release at a reduced price. It is reduced in price as there is no physical book to produce and distribute. Even more radically, you can access any book that has been digitised – even if there are no longer copies in print. In other words, books that would traditionally have had too small a market to warrant a print run can now be made available to the small number of readers prepared to pay for the download. In some cases, texts with a very small niche readership are made available for free in order to establish the market more effectively for later volumes. This has led some writers and publishers to adopt the trilogy approach to book publishing – the first book is free and the second two may be bought at full price.

To a parent and to a school, the Kindle and other ebook readers are a much more *studious* piece of technology than tablets or smartphones and are less likely to be banned and more likely for a school to have already as an available technology for students to borrow or use. Here is a device *designed* for book reading. It is popular with boys, you can change the font size to suit your eyesight, you can annotate the text with your thoughts, and you can look up words you do not know, instantly. And further, you can put your own writing on the ebook reader – and on others' ebook readers. Schools have really been much more receptive to the ebook reader than tablets as a learning platform. There has been a change, however. Amazon have also created a Kindle App, which means that you can now read any of the books in your library on your tablet, your smartphone and your Kindle, and they are synchronised so that if you read to a certain page on one device it automatically goes to that page on another device. Parents can share a library with their child through having more than one Kindle or Kindle app on the same library, and the whole process can be very positive. We are seeing, however, young people perfectly happy to read a text on a backlit screen – such as those found on the tablets – against the e-ink, non-backlit screen of the Kindle. This means that tablets are fast becoming the device of choice for a young person to access reading matter.

Auditing the students and informing the parents

The first point of inspiring your students with use of mobile technology is to ascertain access to devices in a particular class. A simple class or department audit will give you access to this information. In addition, you might offer guidance to parents about your philosophy and approach. If you will allow Kindle ebook readers but not tablets to be used in school then let parents know this. If you are intending to allow students to use mobile technology in the classroom then draw up a set of strict rules setting out their usage to reassure parents that their expenditure will be properly catered for. If you are in a school that is going to invest money into mobile technology then the same rules apply. What additional devices does a student have? May they bring their iPad mini into the classroom and use this instead of the iPad you have provided?

You should refer to Chapter 5 on student safety as well to ensure that safe practice is observed. A policy for a school in which every student is provided with a tablet or allowed to use mobile devices in lessons might look like this:

Mobile technology policy

1. All mobile technology brought to school should be contained within a suitable protective case capable of being dropped or subjected to the usual robust life of a student.
2. Students will be told by the teacher at which points in the lesson they may use their smartphone, tablet or Kindle ebook reader and for how long. At all other times, all mobile technology should be stored within its protective case and placed in the student's bag.
3. At all times, mobile technology should be placed on 'do not disturb' setting or equivalent for that device.
4. Students whose devices emit a sound or alert in contravention of rule 3, will have the device confiscated and placed within the school safe for collection by the parents.
5. All devices will access the internet through the school's wi-fi system which routinely blocks access to inappropriate content.
6. All usage of mobile technology must conform to the school's esafety policy – available here.
7. The purchasing of paid-for apps or in-app purchases through the school's wi-fi is banned – all apps must be free at the point of installation and only the free parts of apps with in-app purchasing may be used.
8. During group sessions, you may be asked to share your technology with your peers – you do not have the right of refusal, only a teacher may decide.
9. If you are using another person's technology, you must be respectful of this property. Failure to do so will result in a ban in using others' technology and a parental interview.

Convergence in mobile technologies

At this point, you can now consider what type of inspirational work you can undertake with your students. The point of this book is not to tell you which mobile technology or apps to use, but rather to enable you to place a structure on your students' use of mobile technology in your classroom or playing field.

Once you have set out a clear and safe approach to how you are going to use mobile technology in the classroom, playing field or indeed outside the school's premises then you can begin to think about how to create opportunities to bring the use of mobile technology into the students' learning as part of your subject delivery. One of the main ways you can approach this is by considering the notion of convergence. Convergence has transformed the ability of mobile devices to compete with the once powerful desktop PC. The desktop PC is the opposite of mobile technologies; it is a large, non-mobile piece of equipment that nevertheless retains a strong presence in schools and workplaces. However, if every time you wanted to use technology in your lesson you had to arrange for a room change to the ICT classroom then you would begin very quickly to get fed up with looking for opportunities to bring ICT into your teaching. Instead, what you need to consider is where tablets, smartphones and other technology such as mini-cameras have started to offer some of the capacity that you traditionally would have gone into the ICT room for.

An inspirational teacher who uses mobile technology effectively will think about if they are offering too much specialist software and hardware to their students for a particular activity. Many people successfully type on their tablets – either through the touch screen or through a bluetoothed keyboard. They use very low-functioning and free notebook-style apps to gather their writing. Some of these apps offer the ability to mix handdrawn or handwritten content alongside typed content and pictures. Although the app is not an 'Office' suite and does not offer a full-size keyboard, the convergence of handwritten, handdrawn type and pictures into a format that can be immediately saved and shared in the cloud offers more potential flexibility. It also offers opportunity to students who have difficulties with managing their work. Students with dyspraxia or dysgraphia, who can struggle to offer neat and readable handwriting, can type the written parts of in-class work but still have the versatility and flexibility that the traditional paper exercise book offers.

Reinventing the wheel

The inspirational teacher might also look for opportunities where they would not ordinarily bother to take the students into the ICT room. Take mindmapping as an example. The concept of taking information and then laying it out into a range of logistical shapes and organisations is a solid learning tool used by all good teachers. Students learn how to sort, synthesise and compartmentalise information across a range of areas. There are any number of very good, paid-for, pieces of software available for the desktop which the school could pay for and install on all the desktops, and a teacher could then arrange a room booking in order for the class to enjoy the experience of using the software to lay out their information. And the truth is that this does not happen. The school will not like the expenditure of putting the software on the desktops, the ICT team will not like the task of updating the software every time an update becomes available and the teacher cannot be bothered to organise a room change each time they want to do a mindmap. So what actually happens is the students continue to lay these things out in their paper exercise books. Yet, when these students finally go into the world of work or university, they find there is an excessive jump in learning needed to start using software to manage large sets of data or project-management software such as Gantt charts or RMstudy. In no way is their time in school preparing them for the world of work – and this is something that we need to address when we teach our students in the classroom. However, the inspirational teacher who likes to use technology can see a way through this. We know that all screen-based mobile technology, whether it be a smartphone or a tablet, will offer a range of free, easy-to-use apps that will happily offer any number of ways to lay out information.

We also know that different students like to lay their information out in different ways. Some like to use tables, some like to use mindmaps, others use a range of flowcharts or a mix of text and images. Thus the inspirational teacher will first train the students to assess the different apps available and learn how to choose different apps and layouts for different types of data. Second, they will consider the technology availability situation: do the students have access to mobile technology in the classroom or not? If they do, then they can build this into the lesson. At a certain juncture, students can add to, share, peer assess or upload to a shared area their information laid out in whatever form they have chosen alongside reflection and assessment. If, by way of contrast, the students do *not* have access to mobile technology in the classroom then the inspirational teacher can adopt the flipped classroom principle and ask the students to collate the information into an app outside lesson time as part of their homework. This enables the school to facilitate a small stock of mobile technology and make it available for those students who come from disadvantaged backgrounds and thus enable them to participate in flipped classroom activities.

At a simple level, an inspirational teacher can use mobile technology to improve a current learning activity. For example, it is quite common at the end of the lesson for teachers to have students write down a summary of what they feel they have learned in the lesson onto a Post-It and to stick this on the wall on the way out. First, this method draws only from short-term memory, so you have no way of knowing what the students are really retaining in terms of their learning; second, here is an activity that could be done electronically. Why not ask the students to tweet or to post to a text wall online what they think they learned in the lesson – but don't make it available until four hours after the lesson? This would force the students to recall the lesson, summarise it and then place it into some form of electronic response thus helping to push the learning into the long-term memory.

What we are seeing, then, is that the inspirational teacher does not look to see how more work, or extra work can be created through mobile technology. Instead, they look for more efficient methods of doing the same work or methods that will improve the learning over and above what they were doing before. This is what excites students – a teacher rationalising to their class that less work and more learning will occur through their innovative use of technology. Remember what we said about the scale of students – some will be technophobes, some will be technophiles, but the majority will be on a line in between.

As a teacher, you need to be delivering a strong rationale at all times to your students as to *why* you are using certain pedagogies and related technologies in your teaching. Students are usually very helpful with this sort of thing and, with your encouragement, will offer ideas and experiences based on their knowledge on how further software and technologies could be brought into your teaching to help them in their learning. Remember, this information is temporary and you teach your students that this is temporary knowledge and likely to change at any point in time. However, by collating their collective knowledge at any one point in time they can take an evaluative snapshot of the current technological offerings and how helpful they are to them as a class in undertaking their learning.

Mobile technology affects the curriculum and your status as the teacher

Traditionally, the student enters the classroom or playing field with just their sum total of knowledge and perhaps an exercise or text book to supplement their learning. In some subjects, some students might invest in a small, focused, printed reader designed to enhance their learning in the classroom. However, the advent of mobile devices is rapidly changing students' access to knowledge. If you want to be able to do something in Microsoft Word, something tricky, would you sign up for an evening class at the local college and sit a course in Microsoft Word? Of course you wouldn't – that would be a wholly inefficient way for you to learn a very specific skill. Instead, the most likely solution would be that you would search the internet and, quite possibly, an online video website such as YouTube, for a tutorial. In the tutorial, you would learn the technical skill of what it is you needed to be able to do and then you would move onwards. We made this point in the introduction – knowledge has become temporary and transient. The internet has become a substitute for long-term memory and should you need to recall the same Microsoft Word technique but cannot remember, you will simply research it again. How, then, does this notion affect your control over the curriculum as a teacher? It changes the way we are seeing ourselves as teachers and our role. Before mobile devices, it was still inefficient for teachers to organise an opportunity for the students to go to the desktop PC, look up the specific skill or knowledge needed and then return to the regular classroom. If a student raised their hand and asked a question to which you, as a teacher, did not know the answer, how might you respond to this situation? Sending a student off to look it up on a desktop PC is a poor solution. That approach requires extra work and does not fit with the concept of rapid formative feedback needed for accelerated personalised learning. However, with a mobile device, knowledge and skill can be tapped into quickly and easily on demand. The long-term memory of the internet is being brought into the classroom.

Should students really use mobile devices to learn?

Many people discuss and debate whether using mobile devices to learn is a good thing. We can look at calculators and see that students do not rely on their mental arithmetic skills, rather, they rely on the calculator for basic sums. However, this argument is reductive. The reality is that mobile devices are here; banning them will not stop students from using them in their own lives or at work. Instead, start to think about in them your subject; whether if you took the student outside school they would still be using a mobile device in some situations. For example, let us take a very simple example of a student writing some poetry.

If someone wanted to create a poem they would have to consider a range of things: vocabulary, style and form, poetic devices and themes to name but a few. Would you have any objection to such a person consulting a thesaurus or dictionary as part of their vocabulary work? Well, such things exist in a mobile device but are far more searchable and comprehensive than the paper versions you find in regular classrooms – so the mobile device is superior to the paper version in that respect. In terms of style and form, someone might need to remind themselves of the different forms available, from a Petrarchan sonnet to an English sonnet, and how they are constructed. Of course, this information is undoubtedly available in some reference books, but you would surely not object to someone looking at a range of sites online or using an app that lets you place words within a predefined structure and check whether the structure is correct or not. Again, the mobile device is quite capable of delivering this information and, in addition, enhancing the skill of managing the metre and form to be correct. You then move on to poetic devices – of which there are a huge number. Really, the best way to understand a poetic device is to see an example. Often, if that example comes from an established and famous poem then that makes it easier to see in context and emulate the device and its effects. The difference, perhaps, between repetition and analepsis (another form of repetition) might be difficult to appreciate without a strong example of each and how they are different. Lastly, thematic topics can be drawn from a range of places and inspiration, and a poet might look at topical news or write around eternal themes present in many successful poems from the canon.

The resulting poem would be fairly successful and, of course, all of this requires no teacher and indeed a teacher would be labouring to *provide* all of those examples and samples. Even further, there are areas in which a teacher simply cannot compete with the internet for examples and sources. While a poem does not have to rhyme, many poems, in fact, do. Why should your student poet not use an app to help them rhyme the lines in their poem? Yet, the poet and the poem *could* be more successful with a teacher around. Indeed, if there were a teacher guiding the student through the range of resources available through a student's mobile device then the end outcome would be a much more successful and independent poet. Thus, instead of the teacher trying to spend an inordinate amount of time teaching a predefined range of skills and knowledge, it might be better if they start to consider how much of their curriculum teaching can be transferred to the mobile device and how much can remain in the classroom.

Expansion of the curriculum

Traditionally, if a teacher wanted to teach knowledge, they would have to have access to a published resource that they could then either buy multiple copies of or photocopy sections of ready for teaching. The installation of projectors and interactive whiteboards has meant that information that is in the public domain can be placed on large screens in the classroom as an aid for teaching. However, it is restricted to the information that is sourced by the teacher and is not personalised to individuals, but suitable for their age group or ability group generally. A school curriculum usually remains quite static with the right of the government and teachers to choose the curriculum enshrined within national curriculum strategy documents or examination specifications. However, with mobile technology, a marketisation of the curriculum occurs. A student in the lesson can access alternative instruction and knowledge to that being offered by the teacher in the lesson. They could justifiably argue that what they are doing is supplementing their learning as well as developing their subject knowledge and multitasking. The teacher is no longer the font of all knowledge, neither is he or she indeed the provider of all knowledge – with mobile devices, the student is bringing their long-term temporary knowledge device to the classroom to compete with the knowledge being offered by the teacher. This will put pressure on educationalists' efforts to control the way in which students learn. For example, in mathematics there are two competing instructional methods for division: chunking and gridding against traditional long division and long multiplication. If, in a lesson, a student was struggling with one particular method and then on their tablet they found an instructional video demonstrating how to complete the same sum using an alternative method, they might well argue that this is the method that is best for them. Who is to argue that the students should ignore the multitude of instruction they are sourcing through their mobile devices? Far better to seize the agenda and instruct the students to *evaluate* the quality of instruction they receive through their mobile devices.

Personalisation of the curriculum

Mobile devices can be used as a specific source of personalisation. A student can access knowledge that they are interested in or need right that very moment. They can receive personalised formative feedback through an app or website that is designed to offer feedback to users on their learning or skill. And all of this can occur in the lesson at the same time as regular teaching. In the same way that the traditional image of a student is one carrying a dictionary, thesaurus and a range of textbooks, so the modern image is of a student carrying a mobile device. Within this mobile device is not just knowledge, but apps that are capable of teaching and providing feedback. In some circumstances, they can provide that knowledge or feedback better than a teacher can. In some cases, they can provide instant and personalised feedback to the student that is beyond the workload capabilities of a regular teacher. Indeed, the larger the class, the more impact mobile technology can have on personalising the curriculum and learning that can take place in the classroom alongside the teaching they receive ordinarily as part of arranged lessons. If students are using technology to help the personalisation of the curriculum and the learning styles, then this is much more like what they are doing at home when they are accessing information and communities through their devices. In addition, it better prepares them for the world of work where everyone from plumbers to office managers will use mobile technology to enhance their personal ability to do their job to a high standard.

Name: Sam Cain
School: Vandyke Upper School and Community College.
Age phase: Upper school; year 9–13
Your role: English teacher.
Types of technology: Laptop computers with Windows 7 installed, internet access a necessity, a Word document with the capability to add comments to it.

Why I developed the idea: I am currently trying to motivate a group to read more examples of creative writing, especially third-person writing. I am trying to motivate them to not only read but have an opinion on whether they like the piece and why/why not.

What was introduced?: Students were given a set of simplified success criteria from the WJEC exam board relating to the creative writing assignments. Students had to go online to www.writingclasses.co.uk/StoryFrames and they had 15 minutes to read as many of the short stories as possible. They were encouraged to stop reading and try something else if they were not engaged with it after five lines. The students then had to copy and paste a personal favourite into a Word doc and annotate the story with comments according to the success criteria. These were then saved into a communal folder on the school network and they could all look at one another's comments.

What problems or successes were there?: I had not seen the group so transfixed while reading in a long, long time. Student engagement was 100%. They were able to see exactly where and how a story could be made engaging and exciting and quickly picked out why it was that they liked or disliked a certain piece of writing. The students found that they found motivation for writing their own pieces. The only problem I found was that the students would have spent the whole hour lesson reading and not assessing anything. Peeling them away from the short stories was a task that had to be carefully and firmly enforced.

What are the next steps?: I will share my successes with the rest of the department at the school and use similar strategies with other year groups and sets.

Advice to other teachers: Don't be afraid to try using laptops and more loosely focused lessons. Sometimes, it works well to let a group like mine just experiment with words. They'll discover that they have personal tastes and that they can write confidently and that they have a style of their own. A style of their own that can enable them to gain marks.

CHAPTER 4

Developing interactive students

Chapter summary

Let the students do the work
The future is here – interactive students in your class
Students are already interacting to help themselves perform well
Recognise and improve the students' current online social networking through behaviour for online learning
A typical interactive student
Compete with their social networking by offering your own online learning
Lifelogging
Lifelogging in your subject
Engaging interactive students

Let the students do the work

The notion of 'interactive students' is the key to all the work you do to inspire your students through technology. The central message at all times must be that if your immediate thought is that it is too much work then you are approaching the idea of using technology to inspire your students incorrectly. In the same way that you do not make your lessons too teacher led, in which you spend the whole lesson providing teacher talk and drowning the students with your own resources, you should also not make your use of technology too teacher led or facilitated by resources created and sourced by you. Instead, you should see your role to be that of the person who provides the structure and security of the environment within which your students interact. Remember, your students will already be interacting online within their own social networking environments. Your job is to harness some of this skill set and bring it to bear in a way that drives learning and interest in your subject. Thus, some of your work is already done – the students are already interactive. They may only be uploading inane videos to their social media stream and commenting on one another's exploits, but it is not a huge leap to have students doing exactly the same thing only *in your subject*; and for their constructing and commenting to be much more learning focused.

The future is here – interactive students in your class

Some teachers might be reading this book due to frustration with their school's approach to technology, whereas others might have been placed outside their comfort zone by a combination of the school's approach and a sudden increase in the level of interactivity they are seeing among their students. It is interesting to note that some teachers have been shifted into having to change their practice to accommodate interactive students due to their school's bulk buying of tablets for all students. Faced with an entire class armed with tablets, a teacher is mandated to create activities in which the students have to use this resource in the lesson. If they did not, the students themselves would soon be making their own suggestions on how the teacher could be emulating other teachers in the school and eroding the notions of respect and power that are central to teaching. Students could well be exposed to a whole range of interactive activities throughout their lessons in the day. A physical education teacher might have students recording instructional elements of a particular move within sport or gymnastics. A geography teacher might have the students gather data onto a central area during a practical activity. The science teacher might use the tablets as interactive exercise books, enabling the students to log their experiments and provide peer feedback as well as receive teacher feedback. Then they arrive to your lesson – what are *you* doing to help these students learn?

Regardless of your school's circumstances and policies towards the purchase of ICT equipment, you cannot escape the fact that your students are already interacting through technology and perhaps even about the work that you do in the classroom! You will be aware that your students are in communication with one another through social networking and that, while ordinarily this will be mostly about social situations, humorous videos and buzzfeed surveys on which films they have watched, there remains a space in social networking for learning.

Students are already interacting to help themselves perform well

If a student were unsure about a part of their learning at home and they wanted to contact a friend to ask their advice, they would not write an email. Young people's use of email has plummeted in the face of social media – they see it as an inefficient way to communicate. Instead, the young person will simply post a message on their social networking feed for each and every person in their network to read. Each young person has a 'stream' of messages on their social network page and they choose which messages to interact with. If, for example, a student in Year 10 was working on their project–let us say they were doing some work for the GCSE geography and were unsure how to do something and Google had not provided the answer–they would post a question on their Facebook or Twitter stream. Something like this:

> Anyone know what the difference is between compound and comparison graphs and which one I should use for the energy homework we've got this weekend?

The range of answers could come from adults or students who are within that student's social network. It might be the student is Facebook friends with an uncle who knows the answer to the first part of the question. The second part is specific to their class and teacher. In this case, a school friend might write what they think they should do. Other school friends from the same class might then start writing how they have approached the same homework. A discussion would ensue in which the group's perspective on the correct way to approach the homework would be established. Come Monday morning, the geography teacher will be presented with a range of homework from the class in which he or she will think either lots of them have got it correct or lots of them have got it wrong. However, he or she will be wholly unaware that there was a discussion happening over the weekend in which the homework was discussed and extra learning took place – unless the students themselves present these facts to the teacher, explain the discussion that took place and ask for clarification as to the correct answer.

As a teacher, you need to be aware that this 'hidden' learning is taking place every night as students and their peers (and even the adults in their lives, such as parents) across the country liaise to help one another improve their work. You cannot be part of their social network to monitor this learning and neither are you expected to. However, you need to be aware that this is what your students are doing so that you can begin to harness those interactive skills and learning that are happening online. At the same time, you need to be aware that some of your students are missing out on this support provided by students who do use social networking. This is important because this exclusion scenario is taking place all over the country with lots of young learners of varying age. Have you considered what happens to those who are *excluded* from such online learning? In the same way a student is at a disadvantage if they grow up in a home with limited cultural capital, so the same is true for the student who has limited social networking. They cannot post questions or get expert advice as part of their online interactions in the same way that their more well-connected peers can. Thus, there are a range of questions and themes you need to consider about your students and their interactions and how they might be missing out from this extra learning that is happening outside school:

- What if there is a student who does not participate in Facebook or social networking?
- What if they are someone who does not have any learned people in their Facebook group to offer advice as a 'learned other'?
- What if they have very few Facebook friends who are in the more able band?

- What if all their Facebook friends are fellow Polish-speaking EAL students?
- What if their autism prevents them from making strong online relationships with others?

It should be immediately apparent to you that some of your students could make better progress if they had more opportunities to interact online successfully around key learning concepts from your lessons. In addition, you should also begin to see that one of the ways of developing interactive students is going to be your awareness that this is one of the 'hows' for *how* your learners collaborate to problem solve. They do not write a single message to a single person. They engage in a multiple-person narrative in which different people will offer different opinions and resources until the group is happy with the answer. If there is no one in the group to offer the 'correct' answer, then a member of the group may approach a teacher or additional learned other to find out a definitive answer. Being aware of this means you can refer to this learning style in your lessons. You can encourage the online sharing of ideas and engagement to the point where you might instruct your students to post questions on their social network sites. At this point, you should be thinking, 'if only I could recreate that online discussion in my own VLE then I could ensure all the students are participating in online learning.' And you would be correct – Chapter 6 on eportfolios and VLEs will help you to do this, but do not think that you can control or prevent the online learning that is happening through Facebook and other social networking sites. You will not be part of their online social group and you have no need to be aware of the latest social networking apps. Your role will purely be focused on two aspects: promoting safe and healthy practice and trying to draw the transferable skills away from their personal activities and into focused learning opportunities.

Whatever your thoughts on the value or status of online social interaction, it is happening and it will continue to happen. The only way forward will be to acknowledge it and to try to influence it (and its use by your students) for the better. One of the ways in which you can do this is by adapting some of the ideas of behaviour for online learning that we have developed as a theme in this book. In acknowledging and recognising that the students might be interacting with one another about the topics you have set as homework or have been discussing in class, you might adopt affirmations and instructions within your lessons that recognise and validate the online learning that is occurring among the students' social interactions.

Recognise and improve the students' current online social networking through behaviour for online learning

In the same way that you encourage your students to help one another as part of their learning, so you can do the same with a recognition of how they are behaving for *online* learning. In addition, consider the different types of student you have.

If you set some work to be done outside the classroom, tell the students that you know that some of them will be posting certain questions on their social media streams and that others will be helpfully answering them. Ask them to consider the quality of their answers, encourage them to post links to resources and even to reflect on whether they have obtained information orally from another learned other, such as an older sibling, and to include this in their online postings. You might have success criteria that the students form themselves on what helpful online interactions look like. Encourage the more able to comment and provide links to resources if they see such discussions in their social networking streams and to take on that role of learned other with maturity and responsibility. At all times, ensure your students know and replicate safe online practice in keeping with the points we make in Chapter 5 on student safety. Encourage key students to contact you through approved online channels if they are unsure about something. This is something that frequently occurs – a student reports to the teacher that there is an ambiguity in a social networking discussion and then the teacher provides the student with a clarification to be placed by the student on the social networking stream for the other students.

Many schools' VLE systems have a means for contacting the teacher. While we know teachers are busy people, there is no escaping that more and more of their teaching is going to be through online management of learning. Certainly this means understanding that, outside school hours, you may have to be available to manage clarification questions from a group as opposed to single emails from single students. This speed is a development of assessment that is clearly happening through having more interactive students and teachers. Formative feedback that is quick and personalised is much more effective than feedback that is quite generic and criteria based as well as some time after the event. Students who are working online, perhaps collaboratively, may be at an impasse unless they receive feedback to clarify matters.

A good analogy would be in considering a traditional non-technological piece of homework – in particular, a vague and poorly defined piece. In response, the teacher would usually receive a variable range of homework submissions depending on how the different students interpreted the task, alongside some non-submissions from students who were too unsure. The point here is that there would be a marked reduction in learning. The students who incorrectly interpreted the task may have produced some work but will not have *learned* very effectively. The students who produced nothing would not have learned anything! If it were possible for the teacher to have intervened and clarified the task before the submission day, then more students would have correctly interpreted the homework and thus more learning would have taken place. This confusion is not an unusual situation and frequently happens in schools. The teacher who engages with their interactive students and encourages students to interact with one another to find a clarification is going to be in a position to increase the amount of successful learning that takes place outside the lesson environment.

Having said all of this, while they are doing well to use their social networking channels to help them with their learning, it is a very distracting environment in which there will be frequently opportunities for confusion or incorrect learning. It is much better to set the agenda and to put into place behaviour for online learning strategies that reduce the likelihood of confusion and poor learning. As before, this may mean that you begin to revisit how much time you allocate to physical paper-based assessment and formative feedback and transfer some of this time to provide formative feedback online instead. Do not try to do online assessment in addition to all the paper assessment you did before as this will be inefficient – you want to be using your time more effectively through ICT rather than creating more work.

A typical interactive student

Let us consider a typical student now. Place to one side the notion that some students do not have access to certain technologies as they come from disadvantaged backgrounds. It may be that, at the end of this book, you will seek outside funding streams to provide technology for such students. However, for the moment, let us try to consider a typical student. And here we need to be careful, since technology becomes obsolete very quickly. Instead of describing which specific software or technology our typical student uses, we need to try to conceptualise it in a way that can cope with the rapid changes in technology and software and their popularity. What is popular and common this year could be obsolete and out of date next year. It is better to accept that this constant and rapid change means not just accepting that everything will be updated rapidly, but assuming that it will be so. So, our typical interactive student then:

- participates in online *friendship-based* interactions through popular and changing social interaction software and apps
- additionally participates in *activity-based* non-friendship communities
- accesses this interaction through a range of devices both mobile and fixed
- frequently changes their mobile technology to take advantage of new apps and tablet/smartphone capacities
- captures audio, photographs and video and stores these online
- comments on others' audio, photographs and videos as well as their own
- owns mobile devices that capture GPS and other statistical data and stores these online
- accesses learning outside the school day as part of their online interactions
- develops temporary skills and knowledge as part of short-term problem solving
- participates in group learning as part of collaborative problem solving through online social interaction.

If this is a typical student, how can you as a teacher start to harness this information to inspire such a student in your subject? Your first thoughts should be centred around the notion of transferable skills. If this is what a student is *already* doing, then it will not be hard for them to do something very similar for your subject in and out of your lessons.

Compete with their social networking by offering your own online learning

Try to compete with the online interactive learning happening through Facebook and other social networking apps and websites by creating project pages on the VLE or some other secure commercially offered service and directing students to present their work online within this space. Generally, you have to accept that whenever you see a young learner outside schools these days their faces are often pressed up close to a screen of some kind. Being aware that this is not all gaming and online chat, but actually contains learning, is the first part of being able to inspire your students with ICT. Engaging with the students, knowing that they are doing this and advising them on how to improve the quality of their online learning through such engagement will have a strong effect on young people who respect you as a teacher and who appreciate that you are not dismissing their online social interaction as valueless and a non-learning opportunity. Just as English teachers recognise that reading magazines is still reading of a high value, so having teachers who recognise that students use social media to improve their learning is going to foster an improved relationship between students and their teachers.

This notion of understanding what your students are up to in their own life is very important for you to be able to harness such activities to the cause of your subject and to be able to inspire them to bring their interactive habits outside the classroom into their understanding of your subject. For example, many students and adults now collate data about themselves constantly; this has become known as lifelogging.

Lifelogging

While not every school will have tablets for every student, the notion of this idea of a student always in touch with their online identity and interactions will help you consider how you inspire your students. Frequently in today's society we see the proliferation of the concept of lifelogging. People of all ages are logging and reflecting on incidents in their life through either social networking or specifically designed apps. However, they are going beyond just taking photographs or writing reflections; they are using these apps to gather tracking data provided by their personal activities. Sleep patterns, GPS data, heart rates, lifestyle pictures and videos, diet, exercise, reading statistics and many other forms of data are either automatically gathered or meticulously entered into data-storing apps. A runner would track their running habits through a GPS device, download the device into a designed website or app, such as Fetcheveryone.com, and then share these statistics through a social networking stream, encouraging discussion among their friends, runners and non-runners alike, who would offer advice, opinions and general encouragement. The idea of the 'loneliness of the long distance runner' has gone. Today's interactive person is bringing a, perhaps, solo hobby to their friendship group, fellow advocates and family. At any point in time, this group of people are not just aware that one of their members is engaging with an activity; they would see videos, photos, statistics, written reflections and also celebrated minor and major achievements with this person as they progressed through the year. However, a physical education teacher might be wholly unaware that this is how the modern runner or athlete engages with their peer group of runners and friends through a combination of lifelogging and online social interaction. The difference between the two is clearly inspiration. It is much easier to sustain your interest in an activity such as running if you know that you can use technology to help bring your own online community to interface with your lifelogging data.

As a teacher, you need to think laterally about how this notion of lifelogging impacts on your subject and how you can use this information to inspire your students. Consider this: if you were to think of someone's hobby, there will be a lifelogging app to help that person gather data. If someone enjoys birdwatching, then there will be an app with pictures, sounds and the opportunity for the birdwatcher to log their own pictures and sightings as well as tweet or send to Facebook their latest activities. Beyond the individual will be the ability to interact with other users of the app – these other users thus become a second group of people outside the online friendship group of the user. Sightings of specific birds will be GPS tracked and logged with photographs as the group starts to function more as a community. The quality of interaction within the app community will be far higher than that of within the online friendship group. The community will be populated with a range of people, from inexperienced newcomers to experienced users, with a background in the area of birdwatching. Any discussions will thus be at a far higher level, and the degree of learning taking place will be accelerated by the individual app user having access to so many learned others from within the field.

Taking that mindset to your own teaching is the next step. If you imagine your own subject, you can start to think about how your students function as a community and how you are using ICT to help create the interactive student. Your class is like an online community of users within a specific subject. Some of these users will be more advanced than others, but there will always be one member of this group who will be taking the role of the learned other – you. In addition, you are aware that some of these students are lifelogging on a regular basis and that this is something to be encouraged – they can generate opportunities for learning through their lifelogging. At the same time, with student safety paramount, you can demonstrate good practice and habits in the field of lifelogging and the sharing of data. In Chapter 5, on student safety, what you learn is that you need to demonstrate good practice in the classroom or playing field so that the students employ these practices in their own lives and not just in school. If you or your school are avoiding the whole issue then this leaves your learners unprepared for the real dangers that exist outside the school. You can *tell* them all the time in class not to do things, but, in reality, the best method will be to have them behaving safely with you in your secure interactive environment and learning how to operate safely in all online environments; this will enhance their chances of being safe outside school and when they are older.

Lifelogging in your subject

Artefacts

Start to consider what artefacts are gathered or created as part of your subject. Where are you storing these? Can the students see one another's work? If you are a history teacher and your students create a reproduction of a historical artefact, can you have them take a picture of it (or scan) and then upload it to a specific area? Have you created a blank project page for this particular topic or study where the students can put a record of their work? Do not get obsessed with ensuring that the work shows a record of assessment. This can happen at a later point. You might ask the students to take a picture of their work and upload it prior to submitting a hard copy to you. However, the notion of letting the students do the work remains – all you should be doing is creating a blank project page within the VLE and directing the students to uploading their work on it.

Numerical statistics gathered as part of their exploration of your subject

Once you are aware that your students are generating numbers, both within your lessons and outside your lessons, you can begin to incorporate these numbers into your lessons to enable the students to reflect on them. Some students will find this easier than others; others could be quite imaginative in their use of this area. Art students, for example, could freely walk around a gallery and then track their pace and time using GPS tracking before matching this up to the actual art gallery's work on display and then producing work in response to the most popular work in terms of time spent and visits. The notion of how curation embraces technology could also be part of the teaching – students could not only produce work, but start to look at how they track their audience. English students can look at reading statistics and difficulty of vocabulary. Maths students could use tracking data from any of their weekend logging to generate statistical and number work. There is some very clever work that can be done by the physical education department using heart rate sensors and GPS tracking devices to monitor students' external fitness routines in ways that resemble how professional athletes approach their fitness tracking. In all of these aspects you will see a very strong correlation between the real-world, real-life data from students and their studies. This takes the theoretical aspect away from your studies and begins to bring a stronger, more personal sense of awareness to your subject. Students will begin to appreciate how real-life events from their lifestyle can play a functioning learning part in their development. It would not take much before your students naturally start to contextualise their lifelogging using the reflective skills you have developed in your subject sessions.

Assessment for learning between you and the student

If you increase the amount of lifelogging data drawn from the students into your lessons, there will naturally be an interaction between you and the students. Your immediate reaction should be that you simply cannot be expected to comment on and assess all these data: and that is the correct reaction. The students should be doing the work in terms of synthesising, in terms of reduction and in terms of engaging with this range of data. You should have a strong sense of assessment for online learning within your teaching and have a clear sequence of formative feedback:

1. Student self-reflection – the student gives themselves feedback and then shows how they have responded to their own feedback.
2. Peer assessment – the student receives feedback from a peer and demonstrates what they have improved in response to this feedback.
3. Student synthesis and selection – the student selects elements of their work that they are still struggling with for your perusal and formative feedback.
4. Teacher-selected feedback – you select and give feedback on key elements that you track as part of your awareness of their progress in your subject.

Engaging interactive students

To engage the interactive student we need to adopt an approach using ICT to enhance the student learning experience, which sees that using ICT is an active learning experience where transfer of learning takes place. What we are saying here is that students are developing a whole range of transferable skills through their interactions with ICT, but also that you need to be aware that this is happening in order to increase the amount of learning that occurs within your own lessons. What has been learned and practised in one context is taken and adapted by the students for use in another context. This can occur from subject to subject and from home life to school life. For some students, they may see things as part of their exposure to the family business or through their own part-time employment. Knowing that what they have learned in one context will work using the same techniques for completing the activity in another context enables them to see that transferable skills are a viable and desirable part of their curriculum and ones that will prepare them for further study or employment in the post-school environment.

Recognising and validating the interactive student who interacts with ICT both within and outside your subject will lead to a greater development of those specific transferable skills that you are seeking to enhance. This will improve the interactive student in three ways: in their own personal interactions; in their interactions within your subject; and in their use of ICT to interact with other subjects on the curriculum.

> Name: Stacy Hodgson
> School: Stantonbury
> Age phase: 11–16
> Your role: English teacher.
> Types of technology: Social network site, Edmodo.
>
> Why you/the school introduced it: A colleague and I wanted a way of tackling the issue of KS4 students not doing homework and also a way to open up discussions and questions students were having regarding revision. We knew the students interacted online as part of their social networking and wanted to transfer those skills across into the way they worked on their homework.
>
> What was introduced and how: we researched and found a learning social network site called Edmodo. You set up a teacher profile and can then create different rooms for your different classes and then pass on a code for your students to join. We wanted something secure which would also appeal, and the students really engaged with the idea of a 'school Facebook', and the fact you can also download an app for it really sold it.
>
> What problems or successes did you meet?: I found it a great way of setting homework. I would post a practice question or a series of questions on a chapter they had read and they would 'comment' their responses. You can set it so that all can see or so that each response is private, but it was great for giving instant feedback and to incite deeper questioning and it also opened up some interesting discussions. I found that I now had a great homework record for my Year 10s and 11s, and they were developing a much more developed understanding of the texts we were studying. They were also motivated and asking me if I was going to post anything that evening. It meant that disengaged students had a more relaxed and friendly access point to revise and ask questions if needed, and it reduced my homework marking time and motivated me to set more and to challenge them on a much higher level with my questions after seeing the discussions it could open up.
>
> What are the next steps?: The next steps are to roll it out to all of my groups including KS3 and see how we could maybe use Edmodo as a whole faculty.

CHAPTER 5

Student safety

Chapter summary

Set the standards for home in school
Cyberbullying
Reacting as quickly as the cyberbullies themselves
Do not let them retaliate!
Keep secure records
It's all jokes!
BYOD security and safety
Security in a public place
Training your students in cybersafe practice
Common security threats
Code of conduct for mobile and extended learning activities
Designing a code of conduct policy
Transferable skills

Set the standards for home in school

Whenever you propose to do anything with ICT in your school, the first thing someone will say to you is: what about student safety? And they are absolutely correct in asking this question. You should always be thinking about student safety when using ICT as this replicates what is happening outside school when the students are doing similar activities, but in an unregulated way.

At a recent training session, a teacher remarked, 'But it is so risky. Having students filming each other and writing comments – how do we control the risk for this?' The first part of the answer to this question is that students are *already* filming one another and posting comments about other friends. They are doing this in the playground during breaks and they are also doing this outside school in their own time. Every single day they are interacting not just with one another, but also with complete strangers, online and with pictures and video, and all in a fairly unregulated arena. And yes, they are exposing themselves to risk and danger and all of this is regardless of whether you choose to have them undertake a safe version of this interaction in your lesson or not. The second part of this answer is thus that as part of your cyber security policy you should be encouraging the students to do similar activities, but under your regulation and with your well-drilled warnings about safe practice and responsible information management. In this way, when they are doing their own personal ICT activities in that unregulated arena they will be safer and more inclined to replicate the good practice that they have learned while using ICT in your lessons. From another perspective, if you choose *not* to undertake this sort of activity with your students, you are actually *increasing* the risk of your students demonstrating unsafe practice.

Cyberbullying

Developing this theme, you begin to see that within the online digital world we get very similar problems to the outside world. Students bully one another in the playground and indeed, as we know, students bully one another online. Students make rude comments in classroom discussions or fail to follow good behaviour-for-learning principles during group work or performance time in lessons. Online, once again, students do not work well in groups or are rude about others' performances.

Sometimes, these problems are amplified when they are brought online. There is a greater amount of anonymity available online and this is where more bullying can occur. In addition, the students will say really quite hurtful things to one another openly and on a public forum due to lack of maturity or cybersafety training. This can happen rapidly and on a scale that is unprecedented in the physical world and compared to traditional bullying. For example, a student could have their online Facebook account compromised through sharing their password or having weak privacy settings. This could then lead to public display of their private thoughts or photographs with multiple comments from students sharing the said comments or photographs on their own Facebook streams. It is described as 'viral' when huge numbers of people start sharing something online, and thus your young student could be quite suicidal by break time with thousands of people from the same town as well as lots of strangers all being privy to his or her private thoughts or photographs. And therein, you see the power of demonstrating good practice within the safety of the school's VLE. When students interact within an official school VLE, all students will have official logins and the space is supervised by a qualified teacher; when students make inappropriate comments, and they will, you will direct the students to remove them and be able to deal face to face with students about the implications of making such comments. Thus you can see how inspiring your students with ICT is not just about getting them to learn and create safely within school-regulated activities, but how to learn and create in a safe way in their own time in less regulated online areas.

Let us consider how cyberbullying is likely to confront you as a teacher and think about how you can help reduce this and deal with it when it does occur. Remember, being a teacher who inspires their students with ICT means that you know how to deal with the kind of issues being raised by students' interactions with ICT. You might not know specifically how to set the privacy settings in Facebook, but you are aware of the reasons why a student should limit his or her posts to just friends and not friends of friends or the public.

What steps should you take when a child is experiencing cyberbullying?

The first aspect here is to be considering your proactive steps. You should be assuming that students are exposing themselves to the threat of cyberbullying and suffering low-level 'bullying' in the form of jocular abuse through their online interactions. This is well entrenched among real and online friendship groups – and at a certain level and within a tight friendship group this 'bullying' will always be within acceptable boundaries. For example, a student might leave Facebook logged in on their home PC and a friend posts a jocular status while they are not looking: 'I've stopped supporting Arsenal and I've gone over to Tottenham' might be the sort of banter-type incident that could occur. This is known as 'frape' a compound of the word Facebook and rape. Picture-warping software can make a friend appear old, overweight or with blemishes and students might doctor an image of a friend and publish it publically. Again, these are all acceptable as part of the boundaries of the friendship group. A student might edit their own image and then send it to friends via Snapchat – an app that deletes the picture shortly after it arrives on someone's mobile phone. However, these are young people and sometimes they overstep boundaries and they might edit an image inappropriately, put an insensitive frape on someone's Facebook stream or share private images outside the friendship group. At this point, the behaviour is moving into the cyberbullying landscape.

Thus, you need to be aware that mild bullying through frape, editing and manipulation followed by the distribution of digital artefacts – *as part of popular culture and social norms* – is going to be what your students are experiencing in their own interactions. On top of that, you should assume that such cyberbullying accelerates at quite bewildering speeds – *viral speed* to coin a term. This means that a solid and equally fast response will sometimes be needed to arrest the viral speed of the cyberbullying. This rapid and consistent response also needs to be embedded into the school's anti-bullying policy rather than be a separate policy document.

Reacting as quickly as the cyberbullies themselves

The first step is that you and the school need to see that with such speed and quick online reactions to cyberbullying, immediate support may be required and teachers should be ready for such events. You may need to call students in and request that they remove comments from their streams or make content unavailable – there is nothing to stop you requesting this sort of thing.

There needs to be solid evidence gathering as well. Recent legislation in the UK – the 2011 Education Act – gives teachers the right to seize smartphones and to even delete data held on the phone. 'Schools will be able to seize items banned by school rules. If school rules prohibit electronic devices (mobile phones, etc.), these can have files removed before they are returned' (Education Act 2011, p.2). Whether this extends to the teacher *mandating* the deletion of data held in cloud source such as Facebook posts or Flickr accounts will possibly be subject to a legal challenge and clarification. A modern smartphone is as powerful as a computer, and the modern tendency is for all data to be stored in cloud servers so even this point can be seen to show how legislation is being outpaced by modern technology. Current guidance says that 'Staff do not have a right to search through students' mobile phones unless the school's behaviour policy expressly provides for this and the student is reasonably suspected of involvement in an incident of cyberbullying which is of a sufficiently serious nature' (http://www.digizen.org/).

Part of the responsive strategy to cyberbullying may be educational in context. The bully may not have realised that they had been a perpetrator and thus may need education as to the ramifications of such an act.

Do not let them retaliate!

One part of providing immediate support is that staff can ensure that the bullied student does not use online interactions to try to wreak revenge using similar strategies or to respond to taunts or online comments. You, as a teacher, can also counsel the student in changing the settings for their online identity to prevent the perpetrators from having access to their victim. Facebook, BlackBerry Messenger, IM list, etc. are all notorious for having settings set at 'connect all' as the default. Frequently, young people post their BBM code (free messaging) on social media streams telling people to use this code to contact them personally on their BlackBerry. Thus, complete strangers could communicate with a young person who shared their access code publically and increase a young person's exposure to risk. This type of behaviour is typical of the kind of strategy that exposes one of your students to anonymous abuse. Deleting the code and only giving the new code to a smaller circle would be a strong first and immediate step a student could do under your counsel.

If the identity of the perpetrator is known and the evidence readily available – a Facebook post for example – the quickest and simplest method to have it removed from the web is for the perpetrator to remove it. The school could not only have the student remove the content but also any other student who had made any reference to the content also removes this from the web. This means that all the associated comments on the original artefact are also removed.

Sometimes, it may be that you need simply to have good knowledge of what a student needs to do if they face a challenge from having their privacy and identity compromised. For example, there are things that the provider of apps and online programs can and will do. If someone created a false Facebook profile then if the real person contacts Facebook they will delete the profile very promptly. The same can be said for mobile phone operators who have policies and staff detailed to deal with nuisance telephone calls. Email is fairly easy to block – one can block whole domain names or simply individual accounts. It is even possible to block emails that contain certain words. You do not need to know *how* this is done for every single app or social networking program. Rather, you need to know that there will be an online video tutorial showing how to do this and to direct the student to the *need* to adjust their settings via access to these online tutorials.

Keep secure records

Dealing with such incidents means keeping secure records. Those who are bullied can forward emails, show where re-edited images are held online or use screen grabs to gather information from cyberbullying places like chatrooms. Again, there is an educational side to this – upskilling the young person to be better equipped to gather evidence of and prevent cyberbullying is a powerful strategy. And thus, just as a school would run anger management classes or anti-bullying classes, so you could run anti-cyberbullying classes designed to empower those who are at risk of cyberbullying. As a teacher, you should be careful, as always, not to reproduce any illegal material such as underage images and to ensure the policy is to involve police and social services at an early opportunity.

It's all jokes!

Any student safety policy needs to see that low-level cyberbullying is part of youth culture. This does not mean it is acceptable – it is not – but it does mean that sometimes what is acceptable within one cohort of young people, and seen as 'jokes', may be seen as cyberbullying by others. To this end, then, education must be at the heart of any policy. Not just education of the victim, but education of the 'bully'. For they may not know they are a bully and indeed in their social circle they may be seen merely as a 'practical joker'. However, it is clear that with the ease of acquiring friends in social networking, the blurring of social norms can quickly occur and victims can rapidly develop. You might see this as part of your own online activities within the school's VLE and you can then step in to educate the person – explaining to them the impact of what they are doing and the ramifications of undertaking such behaviour online in a less regulated interactive area.

Many teachers have no idea about online interactivity and how it all works. These people may well be in charge of anti-bullying policies and even with instruction may be struggling to properly manage some cyberbullying situations. It does suggest that there is a case for further work to be done in schools and also for you to seek out cybersecurity training if some of this chapter has been quite challenging. If you are to be a form tutor who is advising his or her students how to deal with such situations then you can be sure that you would be better prepared by being educated as to the correct sequences that need to be instigated in response to certain situations. Even if you have to rely on others for the technical knowledge, if you know that a certain action needs to be taken then you can initiate your proactive form tutor strategies with more confidence.

BYOD security and safety

Bring your own devices (BYOD) is probably a new area for your school currently, and as such your school might not have an appropriate policy in place. What we can be certain of is that BYOD as a practice will increase and the pressures on schools to engage in BYOD will grow. To be on top of this, schools really need to formulate their policy before the demand from parents and students forces them into the need to implement a BYOD policy quickly and rapidly without training or time to bed in the framework.

Often, a school's first thoughts for new mobile technology is to create a blanket ban policy, but BYOD offers a range of opportunities, outlined in Chapter 3, on mobile technologies, to enhance and inspire students' learning. For this reason, any policy should attempt to embrace the learning opportunities afforded by the advent of mobile devices into the mainstream.

If your school does not have a BYOD policy, then three things are probably happening:

- BYOD is blocked and your school is losing learning opportunities associated with a learner making use of a BYOD.
- BYOD students are already accessing your school network, with or without your knowledge, and you are not doing anything to ensure that this is being done securely; which brings the risk of virus, malware and Trojan horse applications finding their way onto the school network without the knowledge of the school's ICT support technicians.
- BYOD students are already bringing their devices to the school and using them in school time, but just not in your lessons or when supervised by teachers

It is important, therefore, that a clear policy is in place that everyone signs up to, but at the same time allows devices to be used in a controlled manner that enhances the learning experience and ensures that safe, cybersecure practices are followed. Certainly, in the United States, education authorities are making concerted efforts to develop policies so that their students see their school as technology friendly. A number of schools there have developed their own BYOD policies. To encourage other schools to develop student-centred policies, teachthought.com has a website that offers crowdsourced policy templates.

Crowdsourced means that resources have been uploaded to the website and can be used or adapted by users of that website for free. Remember what we have said about technology – you operate in learning communities all the time. One of these learning communities is 'fellow schools that are dealing with the issue of BYOD'.

You do not have to 'join' the community to do so. Just by reading the following sourced templates for inclusion, and adapting it so that your school can develop a policy suited to your students and location, will mean you are part of the community of practice. If you do adopt and adapt this policy, then do publish in other places so that other schools can use your best practice for their own policy development.

It is important that the policy is clear and easily understandable by students, parents/carers, teachers and school staff. For this reason, the language used is very important as not everyone will be familiar with modern ICT rhetoric. It should also fit on one side of A4 so that it can be displayed easily around the school and in classrooms as well as in the school handbook.

BYOT policy document

Purpose: To clearly and succinctly document our school or education authority's policy for BYOT devices onsite.

Audience: All students, school staff, parents and visiting professionals who access school wi-fi networks and/or use electronic devices to complete school work or self-directed learning or recreational activities while onsite.

Definition: BYOT, an acronym for bring your own technology, refers to any student-owned electronic device used to complete assignments, projects and other work in pursuit of mastery of a documented curriculum in a given content area.

What you may use: A device is prohibited if it is or has the potential to be hazardous to the health of users, staff, or students or to hardware and software owned by the school or students. Otherwise, this means Android phones, iPhones, iPads, Google tablets, Windows phones, BlackBerries and other smartphones and tablets are approved if they allow you to complete your work without burdening school resources or the academic performance of your peers.

When in doubt, ask: Contact a school staff member right away and ask if you're unsure about a resource, network, app or any related device use. We want you to benefit academically from the use of your device without damaging your device or getting yourself into trouble. When in doubt, ask.

Viruses and malware: Device security is the responsibility of the owner. Any device that threatens the security of your device or the software and hardware around you needs to be turned off and/or otherwise corrected.

Other risks: Device theft, password security, damage from environmental hazards and dropping, and interference from nearby devices are your responsibility to prevent, recognise and/or correct.

Jurisdiction: This policy applies to onsite (on school property) and offsite in pursuit of completing school assignments and/or documented curriculum in a given content area.

chapter 5 Student safety

> *Digital citizenship:* Our definition of digital citizenship is the 'self-monitored habits that sustain and improve the digital communities you enjoy or depend on'. Keep this in mind every time you send a text, update a social media profile, share a selfie or recommend a resource to a friend, at school or at home. Your digital actions and behaviour are not only permanent, but deeply impact those around you, even if it's not always immediately apparent how. You matter!
>
> *Training:* Training is not provided for use of individual devices, apps or platforms. One of the goals of BYOT is for you to use a device that you're comfortable with and accustomed to using under a variety of circumstances. If you can't use the device, app or website, try another. Ask your friends. Ask your family. Ask your teachers. There are a lot of great resources out there.
>
> *Bad decisions:* Any device use outside of the documented curriculum goals of a given classroom is prohibited and in some cases punishable by law. Disrespectful communication, cyberbullying, spamming, sexting, copyright infringement, trolling (yes, trolling is bad) circumventing district filters or related device monitoring and other abuses of technology will be documented, possibly leading to the loss of BYOT privileges and enforcement by relevant law enforcement agencies.

Security in a public place

This is an area that is, quite rightly, gaining more and more coverage. Remember what we have said: good practice in schools leads to good practice outside schools. So, to round off this chapter, we are presenting current good practice when briefing your students on a flipped classroom project that may require uploading data in a public place. It is true that much of what follows is applicable to everyday life as well as the education context we are placing it in.

Despite all the security measures that you have on your devices, cybercriminals are becoming more elaborate and cleverer in the ways in which they try to access or steal data. There is currently much concern about the increase of hacking into smartphones in public areas and the subsequent downloading of passwords, bank details, etc., even when a phone is not being used and is just switched on. The more that people rely on their devices, effectively the more vulnerable they become to having their data compromised.

Training your students in cybersafe practice

Here are 10 simple rules for students using ICT devices in public areas with some extended explanations following them:

1 Always use a disposable and easily replaceable free email address such as gmail and hotmail for online communications.*

2 Do not access high-value online private areas, such as your bank account, in public areas.
3 Do not keep your passwords on your mobile device.*
4 Do not save your logins on your mobile devices.*
5 Do not leave your device unattended.
6 Do not enter sensitive information in public areas.
7 Beware of people watching 'over your shoulder'.*
8 Ensure all your mobile devices have up-to-date mobile security software – firewall, antivirus, etc.*
9 For safer browsing, disable JavaScript for all but the most essential sites.*
10 Do not use Instant Messenger (IM) while accessing a public network.

Explaining some of the rules

Rule 1*: The advantage here is that you can close the email address at the end of a project and open a new one for the next project, which stops you getting hacked or spammed.

Rule 3*: It might be convenient for you to have them all in one place, but think how much more convenient it is for the hacker stealing your personal information.

Rule 4*: The fastest way to get into someone's area is, if they have saved the username and password, to key a letter into the username box and a dropdown for all the users names will appear, which are usually linked to the passwords.

Rule 7*: People watching over your shoulder are not trying to remember the password you are keying in. There are probably two of them and they are taking turns tracking the keys and the order in which you are striking them. They will then go away, join up their observations and bingo!, into your account they go.

Rule 8*: Make sure that you install all your software updates to maximise security. Many internet providers offer, free security suites. Make sure that you take advantage of this.

Rule 9*: All the browsers allow you to do this. This will help stop malicious programs being downloaded, and stop those annoying pop-ups when you are trying to look at something.

Common security threats

As always, while we are trying to ensure this book is accessible to those with very little ICT knowledge, it is useful to have to hand some common and key terms that you might meet or be asked questions about in class. Many of the terms are actually metaphorical in their design and thus the term itself represents the action and makes them self-explanatory – such as the Trojan virus, which carries itself into a device *within* another piece of software.

Malware

Actually short for malicious software, this is software used to disrupt computer operation, gather sensitive information or gain access to a private computer.

Phishing

Email fraud scams in which fake emails from official companies are sent to a user and used for the purposes of information or identity theft.

Spamming

This occurs when one person or company sends an unwanted email to another person. Often spam mail used as the carrier for malware or a Trojan virus.

Spoofing

When an email, website or a link pretends to be something that it is not, for example a false website pretending to be a real website – this is spoofing. This often happens when a link is clicked in a spam email and you appear to be at a valid web page. Some 'shyster' sites, sometimes known as copycat websites, are fully legal companies charging users for services that are offered by the official government website for free or for a small charge, such as passport and driving licence applications.

Trojan virus

A Trojan horse is a piece of malicious software (malware) that is hidden within something that purports to be a useful file or software program.

Code of conduct for mobile and extended learning activities

The underpinning philosophy for inspiring your students with ICT is that the activities become student led and, in many cases, designed to take place outside the classroom, particularly if adopting a flipped classroom approach. We believe therefore that some guidance for students who are planning to undertake activities outside the classroom would be of help. Working outside a classroom gathering evidence, or data, for a project requires people to follow a set of guidelines for acceptable behaviour and activity. These guidelines are often called ethics or a code of conduct and are used by a wide range of people in a number of situations. Ethics tend to be applied in a professional context, for example research, medicine, etc., and it will be a good introduction for your students to meet the concept of ethics in preparation for the world of work or further academic study. For this reason, we will try to provide a code of conduct template that teachers will be able to draw from with their students for the kind of innovative activities that we outline throughout the book. It also fits with one of our central themes in this book – the notion of behaviour for online learning. You should be educating students into good habits for learning whether they are in a physical place or an online place – or if they are in both! You might be on a school trip with mobile devices and so it is important that the students consider their behaviour for learning, regardless of what they are doing and where it is.

Designing a code of conduct policy

Location

This indicates where the project is taking place: filming, photography, interviewing, canvassing and, selling items or services being the most common activities.

Location ethics is a very important aspect and focuses on gaining permission to undertake the activity. Obviously, if the intention is to undertake the activity on private land, then the permission of the landowner or their agent will be required. This is normal practice – for example you might be undertaking a project in a local shopping centre. In terms of a school project, this might mean acknowledging publically their permission, guidance or support. Acknowledging partners rarely costs anything, but reaps munificent benefits for the school for future activities. Public areas are usually fairly simple places to work in. It very much depends where the activity is to take place and what form of activity is planned, but it is well worth checking with the local or county authority first. Supporting your student's project enquiry with good briefing notes is a must. Certainly schools are well placed for the most part to gain permission without cost. Taking photographs of public buildings is not a given and certainly police stations, town halls, railway stations, airfields and airports, even from a public right of way, could have risks from a security point of view. Encourage your students to consider whether their location and activity has risks. If it is on a public right of way (a pavement for example), is it safe (risk assessment again) or will it cause a nuisance (commuters trying to catch trains in the morning or returning in the evening)?

Participation

This means the people who your students engage with as part of their project activity. These will be people who are not directly involved in the design, planning or content of the project. Participation could include any form of visual, audio or kinaesthetic involvement.

Participation ethics considers who is going to be involved in the activity, what the activity is and who or what will be affected by the activity (see the section on risk assessment). Does the activity require interviewing people? If this is the case, then there must be an information sheet that tells them what the project is, what is happening with the data collected, that their input is anonymous and explicitly asks for their permission to take part. If they do not want to get involved, then they are not to be persuaded otherwise, as it must be a voluntary participation.

Privacy

This may involve or refer primarily to filming, photographing or drawing people, objects and locations.

Privacy ethics are an extension to some of the possible issues outlined in the location element, but here it is extended to include private property. Although if the activity involves taking photographs or filming people in the street, every effort must be taken to ensure that they are not identifiable or, if they are, that their express permission is gained. Permission will need to be gained for visual imagery of schools, care homes, students' playgrounds and any place where vulnerable people may be located.

Health and safety

What does the activity involve and does it require a risk assessment?

Health and safety ethics are more usually referred to as a risk assessment and you may need to talk to the designated person in your school who is responsible for this aspect to determine the implications here. They will also have a pro forma that you might adapt. This pro forma will refer to the activity, location and participants.

Additional practice

This refers to any issues that may arise but that do not fit into the main categories above.

Additional practice ethics really refers to any aspect that has not been addressed in the previous elements, and might include, for example, travel issues and equipment being used – private or school. Are there insurance issues that might need to be addressed? The message is not to go looking for issues to be controlled, but show that you have considered them and put into place sensible and reasonable precautions to minimise risk.

This can really be assembled into a simple checklist, with a series of headings. It is ideal for the students themselves to complete this and determine how they are going to address the issues identified. This aspect is core to them becoming interactive students and understanding that security has wider implications.

> *School/college/academy:* Name of education establishment
>
> *Student names:* Student or student group members
>
> *Year group:* Class and subject
>
> *Project:* A title identifying the project
>
> *Project outline:* A brief outline of the project – no more than 30 words
>
> *Duration:* Time of day, frequency and duration of each activity.
>
> *Facilities:* Any equipment, machinery, devices required at the point of the activities
>
> *Location:* A brief description of the locations in which the project activity will take place – Public or private – indoor or outdoor, etc.
>
> *Participation:* What form will the activities take at each location? Who will be involved (for example members of the public chosen at random)?
>
> *Risk assessment:* Are there any issues that might affect the group members or participants due to location, activity or materials?
>
> *Additional:* Are there travel issues, permission expenses, safety equipment, etc.?
>
> *Confirmation of adherence to appropriate school policies concerning personal security, safety and behaviour*
>
> *Signed and dated by each group member*

Transferable skills

To end this chapter, we will remind you of our central premise – let the students do the work. And this also applies to student safety. Your role is to reinforce good practice within a safe environment and be training the students to consider ethics, practice and implications of their work with technology. This approach ensures that students think about the issues and elements before they embark on any project activity, and it is this preparation that is a cornerstone of any successful project. There is an emphasis here on distinct learning and meeting skills objectives as it develops both independent learning skills and transferable skills. Particularly for students who are moving from the compulsory sector, this part of the project activity will provide real evidence of soft skills that higher education and employers alike look for. At the very least, their own private interactions are likely to be safer and more responsible as a result of your work with them in your lessons. Do think about a whole-school approach to ICT and then embed student safety within this policy rather than having separate policies and approaches inconsistently around the school. The best schools are ones that have clearly designated people who provide

chapter 5 **Student safety**

support and training as well as leadership across the whole school in their approach to ICT and students safety within the school.

> Name: Jackie Samosa
> School: Mark Rutherford School
> Age phase: Secondary 11–19
> Your role: Assistant headteacher with leadership responsibility for whole school ICT.
> Types of technology: Whole-school policy on technology with student safety embedded throughout.
>
> Why you/the school introduced it: More departments across the school are now starting to embrace technology as they become aware of more innovative practice. Some of it is driven by necessity. For example, the maths department sees that it is no longer competing only locally, but rather that national expectations means that they should be competing with children from other countries in maths. For them, this means they need to be at the cutting edge of learning and technology.
>   Within computer science, they are now starting to get children to program using JavaScript. This enabled the students to use their own mobile phones in class to test the screensavers that they had written. It is all very well having the children write their own apps, but the concept of testing their apps must be brought into the equation. This can only be done if you let children use their smartphones in the classroom.
>   What was introduced and how?: We have brought in the right for students to be able to use their own devices around the school in and out of lessons – as long as it is authorised and part of a constructive learning opportunity. Some staff worried about the idea of letting students use their mobile phones in class for learning opportunities. However, the school has implemented a clear behaviour-for-learning policy around appropriate and inappropriate usage of phone.
>   Some departments have bought some mobile technology for specific students. For example, they have some tablets with the Kindle app for EAL students. There is also a budget for buying books on the Kindle app for the EAL students.
>   We have invested money to purchase the It's Learning VLE platform. The school has adopted the use of inhouse champions who are confident in their use of It's Learning and they put on training sessions for the other teachers. However, the school does not force departments to use it.
>   We have introduced a whole-school improvement plan for ICT. Each subject department has to set out clearly in their own improvement plan how it will use ICT to support whole-school targets as well as reinforce student safety at every step of the way.
>   What problems or successes did you meet?: One of the biggest issues we found in bringing the school forward was the infrastructure issues around

wireless technology. Enabling students to access the wi-fi means more capacity is required to ensure the students can function well. At the same time, it had to be future proofed to make sure that the system would cope in a year or two and not need upgrading again.

Teachers have struggled with the idea of bring your own devices. Teachers see it as a minefield and want to know who is responsible for the devices: theft, damage, inappropriate material, etc.

The school takes esafety very seriously and it forms a regular part of whole-school training. Our view is that students who are using technology safely within school and the school's systems will be more likely to be safe when they are engaging with unregulated social networking and other forms of online activity.

One way the school has used the VLE well is by using the VLE to provide students with quality feedback. They are getting regular high-quality feedback for their work through the VLE. In addition, the school uses the VLE to track submissions and deadlines; thus we are getting much more up-to-date information about a student and their commitment to their work.

There have been some interesting gender outcomes through the deployment of It's Learning in the way that boys are competitive over their work on the VLE. This competitive element is clearly leading to improved learning and attainment outcomes for the boys.

What are the next steps? In summary, the school is delivering the ICT curriculum across the school. We believe that good ICT teaching and planning can avoid overlapping curriculum planning from different subjects. The senior management team has appointed and backed an AHT with whole-school responsibility for ICT across the school and curriculum, and this is clearly the main driving reason behind the school's success in embedding ICT in all aspects of the curriculum and why the school is ahead of its competitors when it comes to utilising ICT to drive forward learning.

CHAPTER

Eportfolios and virtual learning environments

Chapter summary

Managing students' coursework and classwork
Preparing students for technology at their next level of education
Eportfolios and coursework folders
Activities to consider for eportfolios
Virtual learning environments in schools
Look for good practice
Your students attain and achieve differently online from when they are in the classroom
Assessment for online learning
The VLE should be a space in which opportunities for learning exist
Activities to consider with VLEs
What if your school does not have a VLE?
Eportfolios, VLEs and the cloud
Alternative VLEs other than those in your school

Managing students' coursework and classwork

A long-term issue for teachers has been the management, tracking and general assessment of student-created work – especially for assessment. Traditionally, this work can be called things like 'coursework' or 'controlled assessment' and be held in folders or sent to examiners for moderation. Even in younger, non-formally assessed classes, there are still large ranges of individual and group work being produced that need assessing and managing. Some schools are responding to some of the modern changes to qualifications by reappraising their approaches to the management of such work and by using ICT to both inspire the student and to help teachers track the students' work and learning more effectively using eportfolios – best described as online interactive storage of a student's work and learning.

The connection between eportfolios and VLEs

The development of online learning is a natural response to the vast amount of work being done by schools and colleges with virtual learning environments (VLEs). Most schools and colleges have bought into off-the-peg VLE systems such as Moodle or It's Learning. These are designed to both be a place of online learning and a place for students to upload their work for teachers to assess. As software has evolved to take into account the multiple entry points from a range of mobile and fixed devices, so new software packages are coming on-stream. For example, some of the newer VLE or eportfolio packages come bundled with apps for smartphones and tablets in which the student just takes a picture or video of their work and it is automatically added to their eportfolio or area on the VLE in a secure and safe way ready for further reflection and assessment. If you consider the physical education teacher who has to assess really quite a lot of students' performances across a wide range of sports and areas, then it is impossible for the teacher to record and assess each and every student using technology. However, if the students themselves are responsible for maintaining the online folder of evidence through a video record of each assessment stage then it becomes much more manageable for the teacher. In addition, the student is able to review their performances across a range of disciplines and can use their own time outside the lesson to record new and improved performances and can place these in the eportfolio. This would particularly be useful for students who undertake a range of formal instruction outside their school as part of their training through their sports clubs and coaching academies.

Consider students who receive coaching or instruction through an outside agency, such as a drama school, music tuition or a local athletics club and who are delivering performances on a regular basis. Are these data being stored as part of the school's record for this student? It is unlikely. However, an eportfolio area that is maintained by both the school and the student would be a strong opportunity for that type of information to be better stored. Not all learning is undertaken through school, and the eportfolios and VLEs are a good way to blend information from all a student's learning opportunities both within school and outside.

Preparing students for technology at their next level of education

The best way to think about how you can best inspire your students is to consider how they are going to be using these skills at some point in the future. For example, if you go into higher education today, the educational landscape is really quite different from that which some students are experiencing in their schools. Many universities across the world use a special anti-plagiarism tool called turnitin© which scans every piece of a student's work and matches it up with every other piece of student work submitted through turnitin© in all universities *and* all online published content, and then delivers a report to tutor and students on the plagiarism level of their work with every phrase or sentence taken from another source highlighted. To facilitate this, the student's written (typed) work is, by its very nature, submitted online through turnitin© where the tutor electronically accesses the work, marks it online and then makes it available to the student to download and read along with comments.

Some students struggle with the transition to this HE environment because schools are unaware of how the higher education sector has moved on. For some units, on some courses, the students might be asked to interact as a group online to create a resource as part of their assessment. Again, this is something many schools could naturally do as part of their work with VLEs, but if a student has never undertaken such an activity then they are likely to have a poor transition to higher education and struggle to perform competently. By justifying to your students that you are mimicking the type of activities that they are likely to meet in higher education, your students are more likely to be inspired to engage with this type of online interactivity.

Eportfolios and coursework folders

The first thing to think about with eportfolios is to assess hwhether you have large folders of work for each student held in a filing cabinet or cupboard where they are stored until the end of the year or if someone wants to assess student learning. The other thing to consider is if there is evidence of learning that you cannot capture through the traditional folder of work. For example, this might include videos of students in the process of construction as well as videos of finished performance. It might include photographs of students' work and planning in progress. For example, your students might construct and maintain large mindmaps of ideas and learning over several lessons. These might have no individual ownership and individual contributions might be varied; nevertheless they are still good examples of student learning and progress and should be captured. Generally, teachers might struggle with this type of group-work evidence and it ends up in the bin or removed from the board. Frequently, brilliant in-depth whole-class engagement is scribed onto an old-fashioned whiteboard for a matter of minutes before it is wiped off in readiness for the next class or activity. However, a simple set of photographs uploaded to the class VLE would enable each student to not only see the work but also create a reflective piece that they could hold in their personal eporfolio, reflecting on their contribution and learning from undertaking the group work. The same can be said for videos of groups or an individual student's performance. By having it available for review online, you can then build further assessment for learning-related activities around these materials. Students can get used to capturing and reflecting on their learning and performance in the classroom or out on the playing fields.

Immediately, we begin to see our notion of eportfolio is being challenged by the interactive nature of group work, but that with lateral thinking we can start to see how the eportfolio can dovetail with the VLE to create an environment of learning and reflection for not just an individual student, but a group or a class of students.

Activities to consider for eportfolios

- Consider your next lesson in your subject – what processes are at work? What evidence of learning is there that no one is seeing or capturing apart from you as their teacher?
- Are you encouraging the students to capture evidence of their learning? Students often carry a camera as part of their smartphone or tablet. By having students begin to capture work and upload it to secure shared environments, you can build lesson activities around these.
- What evidence is there of progress within the lesson? Over a series of lessons? If this evidence is only in exercise books then it is temporary, often hidden, awkward to access and not in keeping with how these students are going to have to function at university or at work.
- How often do you have students 'reflect' on their learning and what evidence do you ask them to consider?

Virtual learning environments in schools

Schools in the UK have been under pressure to use VLEs for quite a while now – it really started when the UK government published its *Harnessing Technology* report in 2005, announcing that state schools must provide access to a virtual learning environment for all their students by September 2008. However, this was not a successful announcement as it is all very well telling schools that they have to do something, but if you do not roll out training and support then you cannot expect it to be effective. The result is that schools' provision of VLEs is, at best, variable.

An effective school will arrange regular training in which teachers learn not just the technical skills behind operating a VLE, but the pedagogy behind these skills. As this book is concerned with ICT pedagogy, it is better to focus on pedagogy rather than any specific VLE software that is likely to rapidly become obsolete. Whichever school you work in, and whichever VLE you have to use, you want to be using the same type of student-led pedagogy to help you extract maximum learning from the students' use of the VLE for the minimum level of effort on your part.

Look for good practice

The first thing you should consider then as a teacher is looking at where good practice already exists. This may not naturally be at your own school but at a local school. As it is a VLE, it will be easy to arrange an after-school visit to this neighbouring school and have a look at what it is they do with their VLE to help engage their students with learning. What you do not want it to be is just a repository for files or homework. If the school wants somewhere to store files then an online drive or shared drive will be more suitable for that usage. Remember our point from earlier on in this book: if all the student sees when they log into the VLE is 'homework', especially homework that is not actually done online, then you will not be surprised to hear of students who forgot their logins or their internet was not working. A successful VLE is one in which the students are inspired to log in and interact with the environment as it is not only enjoyable but delivers extra learning.

The next place to look for good practice is within your own students themselves. Consider the concept that your students already manage texts, images and video online in an interactive way as part of their digital footprint. This is mainly in the form of social networking through software such as Facebook. However, this is not the only social networking tool, and students are increasingly using applications such as Snapchat and Instagram to interact with each other. You can be sure that new applications will rapidly become popular and old applications less so – this fits with what you are learning about how software comes with a built-in obsolescence. Have high expectations of what your students are capable of doing once they bring their transferable skills from their social networking to bear on your VLE.

Your students attain and achieve differently online from when they are in the classroom

What you will immediately notice on getting students to post their ideas, thoughts and interactions on the VLE will be how their online personas are different from the persona in the classroom. You can use this knowledge to inspire your students – in particular, those students whose online activity is more confident and assured than their classroom-based interactions. For example, let us take the most common method of teaching one finds in the classroom or out on the sports field: the question and answer session. The experienced questioner will seek to develop the students' knowledge and understanding of a topic using a variety of immediate questioning methods. They might adopt a hands downs policy or indeed take a mix of hands up and choosing students in their attempts to differentiate the questions for the right student depending on how hard the question is. They do this as they know that when someone is engaging with a question then learning can be made to happen. The more challenging the questioning, the more effective the learning that takes place.

Now let us consider the teacher who is seeking to inspire their students through the use of the VLE. Within the class space on the VLE, the teacher sets up some discussion forums. Each one is on a topical area that forms part of the question and answer session in the classroom. So we are not replacing the class-based question and answer session – rather, we are supplementing it. However, this time, the 'less than confident' student who likes to be sure of their answer before they engage with a question has all the time they like to consider their answer. Even further, to reinforce their answer they can now cite their source of inspiration using a link to learning or knowledge somewhere else. A less than confident science student might link a video of an experiment to show how someone has completed a basic chemistry transition. Students are no longer guessing in the empty space of the classroom – now these students are actively citing and linking as well as commenting on one another's contributions. Instead of the teacher being the main fulcrum of the question and answer session, more able and confident students will direct and lead the discussion. The place of the teacher as the learned other will be supplemented and reinforced by the group interaction online.

Assessment for online learning

What the online space also offers to the students is a terrific opportunity for peer assessment and peer learning. This means you can employ assessment for online learning principles really effectively. When students upload their work, you should set it up so they have not only to reflect on their own work, but also to write reflection on one another's work. With more time and space for rebuttal, you could see an increase in the quality of AfL being undertaken by the students as part of their work in your lessons.

What we see, then, is that the VLE needs to be a space in which learning and interaction can happen, but within a safe and controlled space that is supervised by a learned other – the teacher. In addition, the teacher and the traditional classroom-based more able students are no longer the learned others. There is a new learned other – the *online student* learned other.

The VLE should be a space in which opportunities for learning exist

The VLE is a space online in which you can build opportunities for learning – not a space in which you place large quantities of information that already exist on the internet. There is no need for you to try to compete with the resources on the internet, and indeed it would be a poor use of your time. Instead, you are training your students to constantly evaluate their sources of information for validity and objectivity and to interact with them as part of the learning opportunities you are offering within your lessons. In addition, you are also creating 'spaces' in which these interactions can take place. This may include areas in which students can place original or reshaped work relevant to your subject.

You might, at this point, feel that students will still need instruction. They simply cannot go online and engage with a whole range of unstructured learning, knowing intuitively what to do. And you would be right – they do need instruction, but not in the way that you see it. The instruction takes place within the lessons that you actually teach. In other words, when you are planning your lessons and schemes of work, you will be thinking about the online spaces that need to be created alongside the scheme of work. In the same way that you prepare a display board ready for a students' work, a spreadsheet for the students' grades and folders for the students' writing, so you create an online 'project space' within which you will place topic headings, discussion forums and places for the students to upload their works in progress and finished products. The technical knowhow of how to do this will be really quite low – most software is designed to be fairly user friendly in the creation of the online workspace for the students. However, if you are doing this on your own it will be hard work as only you and your students are learning how to do this. It really needs to be a departmental approach: everyone in your department needs to utilise the VLE as part of their teaching. In this way you can problem solve how to put the project space up with one another. In addition, the students will quickly learn how to use the VLE as part of their class, and when they move classes it will not cause transition issues as they meet a teacher using technology in a way that they are not used to.

Activities to consider with VLEs

- Investigate what training is available within your school or chain for the VLE.
- Find examples of best practice from local schools – consider a different phase, especially if the school is a feeder school for you. This will enable you to tap into skill sets already developed in the students by other teachers.
- Audit your students to find out what sort of online skills they already have. Can they film and edit videos? Can they create online texts? What apps do they use to create their personal projects? Knowing this information will help you create inspirational lessons which draw on the students' pre-existing transferable skills to get them interacting with learning in your subject.
- Reinforce your current learning activities with online areas such as discussion forums or topic spaces.
- Monitor their online interactions and interject as the learned other to stimulate discussion and correct misunderstandings.
- Build in assessment for online learning opportunities as part of the work structure.
- Work as a department so that there is a consistency of approach.

What if your school does not have a VLE?

What if your school does not have access to any technology relating to eportfolios and VLEs? This does not preclude you from adopting the same pedagogical stance to the way you and your students are storing the work – as long as you run a strict regime over student safety and take into account the different ethical issues around cyberbullying and cybersafety.

One straightforward way to approach this issue could be through an adaptation of blogging. Blogging is an online diary in which people can store text, pictures, videos and links to other websites. The blogger updates these on a regular basis and they decide who can have access to their blog to read what they have written or uploaded. There are indeed free, commercial blogging sites that are appropriate for either individuals or for groups. What you are also able to do is to have multiple users on a single blog. This means, as a teacher, you can have all your students participating in the same blog. This means you can allocate pages for each student and you can ensure all of the student safety is properly catered for. It is also an opportunity for you to showcase the students' online work to school senior management in order to encourage your school to consider investing in a school-wide VLE or eportfolio so that all of the school's students can benefit.

Eportfolios, VLEs and the cloud

We touched on the cloud in Chapter 1, where we outlined what it is and how it is used in ICT. You will find that eportfolios are an ideal area for using the cloud. Much of the traditional work and assessment in schools is carried out in the actual school environment, but the activity and the notes that the student develops in the course of their learning are not always easily accessible to students outside of school. The online VLE linked to good eportfolio space means that a student can continue to work on their entire portfolio of their work and assessment without having to be physically in the school or taking up a teacher's time or supervision. As we have already seen, student access to their files is no longer restricted to the school day, and this is likely to become the norm rather than the exception as technology and education progresses.

This, in particular, is where using the cloud becomes a facility that enables students to access their data whenever they need to (providing, of course, that they have internet access). It is also important to think about the type of mobile device that the student might use and the issues of both accessing the school network remotely and the costs of uploading and downloading their working files. Many smart devices with mobile internet access have limits on the amount of data that can be downloaded and uploaded, therefore it is important that how students access their data is done in a smart way. This is where the cloud, or correctly referred to, *cloud computing*, comes into its own. We outlined cloud storage in Chapter 1 and, in particular, the cloud storage available free from a number of providers, such as Google with Google Docs©, Microsoft with Skydrive© and Apple with iCloud©. For users who perhaps do not use these providers, there are a number of independent cloud providers that offer a basic facility free, which for most student users is more than adequate. Students are able to upload and download files from a secure area and work on them effectively and efficiently with complete confidence in the security. This last point is important as these organisations have the resources to develop and implement security strategies on a scale that schools are unable to compete with.

The service of offering public providers cloud access is known as the public cloud, and this is where a service provider makes resources such as software or data storage available over the internet, with access to the public cloud often inexpensive or free. An alternative for a school to offer similar flexibility but additional control is to use a private cloud. Here the same software and storage can be offered, but access is restricted to authorised users. While this is not free in the same way that the public cloud is, the cost is based on a standard access and facility charge usually levied annually. A significant advantage here for a school is that the costs of security and access are borne by the private cloud provider, thus freeing up the school's own technical support. Also, it would provide a secure entry to the school network, with all the assessment and supervisory features of a VLE such as Moodle. Certainly if a school wishes to develop the flipped classroom concept, which we outlined in Chapter 2, then the use of the cloud will both underpin and facilitate this innovative and engaging approach.

Remember, most students will already have access to some sort of cloud computing. The more we are able to use technology that students are familiar with and in a way and at a time most appropriate for the students, the more likely we are to inspire to engage in the learning process. One of the key themes of this book is about using a student's transferable experiences in technology to inspire and engage them to enjoy learning areas of your subject. This clearly goes for cloud computing, and you should be engaging with your students' experiences of storing and editing their work online before you design and implement your own strategy.

Alternative VLEs other than those in your school

So far, we have expounded on how students can have their learning enhanced and accelerated by you developing your usage of VLEs and eportfolios as part of your teaching. However, it is worth considering how this area is developing internationally and becoming a mainstream part of education across a range of geographical and educational landscapes.

In the first instance, some VLEs try to emulate being an educational establishment entirely – being a place in which to learn that has no active teachers arranging physical learning events whatsoever. The reasons behind this development are twofold. First, it is an exceptionally cheap model of education. The second main reason is that because access is not physical, anyone in any geographical location can access these cheap and easily obtained materials. In the same way that an ebook can be reproduced again and again with no production fees, so can the online learning environment offer the same features to multiple students year after year. Instead of a teacher's materials being accessed by a couple of hundred students a year, they can be accessed by hundreds of thousands of students. As the resources are electronic there are no reproduction fees. In addition, the materials can be quality assured and regulated by an approved awarding body.

This is not a new model of learning: the Open University and others have offered distance learning as a strategy for a long time. The difference between distance learning through physical materials sent in the post and materials available online is in the access to materials. All a student needs is online access and some form of mobile or fixed device and they cannot just access materials but start to function within a learning community. This second point is fundamental to the nature of online learning. In distance learning you have to self-study and then send your assessments in or attend external assessment events. With a learning community you can engage with others of a range of abilities. You can begin to interact with people to ascertain whether your learning is of a sufficient standard for the assessment. For example, many communities of online learners are at different levels of assessment but still functioning as a learning community. Many formal institutions, such as the Open University, appoint a paid tutor who will monitor the online learning community and play the role of learned other to clarify things when they are needed. They may simply monitor the discussions and learning boards, but they will also offer formative feedback to students and amend future learning materials based on the events that they see online. While there are very formal and organised public-service-style virtual learning environments, there are also any number of private versions all competing with one another. Whether you would like to learn a language, carpentry or how to knit, there will be a virtual school with a range of resources and an online learning community integral to the learning process.

So how does this affect you as a teacher in a school? Well, these are not just your competitors, but your fellow teachers. They could also be teaching your students.

There is a very good chance that some of your students already access such self-running virtual schools and are learning through online materials. For example, a young person wishes to learn guitar. Physical guitar lessons are expensive, and perhaps the student is not really that committed to regular practice. An online virtual guitar school will have videos, music, activities, forums, peer assessment and feedback and be a strong and engaging regular learning activity for this student. This student may simply be going to their music lesson and engaging in a whole range of musical activities, but if their music teacher was aware that they were undertaking such online learning they might start to engage with the activities the student is doing and indeed start to collate a stronger picture of what learning the student is undertaking. If you recall in our chapter on mobile devices, the curriculum is under a sustained assault from this alternative learning. The teacher, school and government no longer have a monopoly on how and what is being learned by a student in your subject. Instead, the student has the ability to use ICT to explore and develop their learning in ways that they want to *in addition to that which they learn in school*. A teacher who takes an interest in the learning that their student is undertaking as part of a virtual school, one who not only validates it with approval but engages with it, using it to personalise and develop the learning the young person is undertaking in their lessons, that teacher will clearly be inspirational to the student. Instead of hiding their learning or having it ignored, it becomes part of their learning and is joined with that they learn as part of their schooling.

If we expand this way of thinking, there will be some students who need extra tuition for whom these online virtual schools will offer something that they cannot actually readily access. From an international perspective, this might mean instead of being trapped in a social cycle of low education, a young person in another country could access online learning to use education to break out of the trapped situation they find themselves in and forge a new pathway for themselves using the alternative education as the driving force. Some of these international models are known as massive online open courses (MOOCS) and are designed specifically to offer access to education to a whole range of disadvantaged people of all ages and all countries. From your perspective, it might be that your particular students might not actually have access to specific learning opportunities within your school and so you might get your students to look at alternative online virtual schools as part of your lessons. For example, if you are a drama teacher, you might set up a project in which the students access free samples from a range of online drama schools and discuss which ones offer the best value for money and best meet class members' agreed success criteria. Thus, instead of ignoring the range of online learning opportunities available to your students, you are embracing them and then, going even further, you are developing within them a consumer acumen to distinguish between poor-quality learning opportunities and high-quality learning opportunities. It might even be that your school decides to offer its own MOOC, and this would fit with the developmental direction that MOOCs have taken.

You do not have to be living in impoverished conditions to struggle to have access to good education in specific areas. It might be that your students are located quite remotely and thus never have access to *other* students interested in your subject in the way that they are. They may lack the learning community that is needed to make learning engaging and a positive learning experience. It might be that they are in a school in challenging circumstances and have little access to specialist and well-trained teachers in a particular subject area. It could even be that your student is exceptionally talented for their age and they are not getting enough specialist input in your age-specific school. Whatever the situation, there are times when a public or private virtual school could be suitable and recommended. Bearing in mind that student safety, good training and awareness of what a good cybersecurity policy looks like must be at the heart of any access to external online learning opportunities for your students.

Name: David Shea
School: Woodland Academy
Age phase: 9–13
Your role: General teacher.
Types of technology: It's Learning VLE.

Why you/the school introduced it? It's Learning was introduced as the school's VLE, as the headteacher is very keen on the school adopting modern practices to our teaching. We are trying to show how it could be used to enable a more collaborative approach to learning and develop a more effective learning community.

What was introduced and how?: Project spaces were created online for the different units of work within the students' lessons. In addition, online discussion chatrooms were organised during specific evening hours to encourage the students to access one another and the teacher during their out–of-school time.

What problems or successes did you meet?: Many of the students would log in to discuss how to tackle certain aspects of the projects. The chatrooms were more of a success than we expected. However, it tended to be the same students each time, so we introduced some discussion groups that were more specifically focused – such as the more-able discussion group. The project spaces were also populated really quite well, but we need to do more work to establish a good relationship between school-based work and online work.

What are the next steps?: The next steps are to revisit the schemes of work and to consider how we can start to plan more effective online work to dovetail with the planning for school-based work. Currently, our planning is focused wholly on lesson time or homework rather than opportunities for the class to liaise online.

CHAPTER 7

The extended school

Chapter summary

An introduction to the extended school and the online extended school
An extended school with technology requires lateral thinking
Technology means more than just online resources
The extended school is for your students as well as the community
Use the familiar whenever you can
Setting up a video project with the notion of the extended school
The extended school and the flipped classroom
Citizenship, mobile technology and the extended school
Acquiring the media devices

An introduction to the extended school and the online extended school

An extended school is one that considers the range of services or activities that it provides and how well they are matched up to the needs of the local community as well as their students. These schools see themselves as a viable hub of the local community, offering the facilities and expertise needed to ensure that the local community can help itself and its students progress well and enjoy a fulfilled and productive life. Traditionally, this means playing a physical role in the local community by offering wider access to the facilities and expertise of the school. However, the moment you consider how communities function and their access to ICT equipment, you begin to see how possibilities for expanding the notion of extended school can arise.

Technology can play an important role in the extended school because it enables the school to extend its reach beyond the physical confines of the buildings and out into a more online and interactive local community experience. At a simple level, this might simply mean having a good website with lots of helpful information. At a more progressive level, it might offer ways for parents to better support their students through the availability of online interactive materials related to students' study. At an even higher level, a school might start to converge its online offerings with the non-school-based services being offered within the buildings. The local five-a-side football club might get ICT support to better enable team members to interact with one another as part of a learning community. The school website might offer to host the webpages of local groups or services, providing them with the security expertise and simple ICT backroom support that could be challenging to a local group that did not have access to the knowledge needed to source and quality assure these services from the private sector. In addition, having a local group's webpages hosted via the school's ICT provision would attract traffic from both types of user to the same central starting point – the school website. Here, parents would be exposed to updates and interactive opportunities within the school as they passed through the school website in order to access the hosted pages of a local group. This local group, for example a mother and baby group in a nearby community hall, might not actually access any physical part of the school. So you can see how offering the school's physical infrastructure up for the use by the local community can be extended to the notion of the *online* extended school by offering the ICT infrastructure up for the use by the local community.

An extended school with technology requires lateral thinking

Whereas at this point you might be thinking of yourself as a teacher of students, when you start to consider the *online* extended school you have to think more laterally. You begin to think about how your work with technology affects the community that surrounds the school. If all the different sections of the local community receive support from the school to function more effectively, the impact will be felt strongly across all aspects of the community – including the attainment-based outputs and progression rates of your students.

The first step in this lateral thinking is to start to think about the different types of technology that can be used. Why should the five-a-side football team that uses the school in the evening not have access to some interactive resources on football skills? Why should team members not have access to interactive learning packages which demonstrate how they can use their own mobile devices to record and assess their own performance and progress? If the school's students are already producing these resources as part of our repeated theme of letting the students do the work, why can these not be made available to the wider community as learning opportunities and resources for them as well? It may be that both students and the local users of the five-a-side football resources already have familial- or friendship-based connections, and this would help improve the cohesiveness of those connections as well as widen the understanding of how education works in the modern era.

We are not asking you to create, locate and store these resources for the local community – instead it might be that your students take this active role. Rather, we are asking you to consider if learning could take place within both the students who provide such resources and the local community that receives them. Ask yourself, are transferable skills being developed that could be useful for the students or local community at some point in their educational or work-related future?

To develop this theme, it is necessary for you to acquire a theoretical understanding of what your school and students could be doing for the students and the local community through the adaptation of technology to the concept of extended school. Remember, you do not need to be able to use any of this software or these ICT devices. As we have mentioned before, the likelihood is that by the time you have learned how to use them they will be obsolete.

Technology means more than just online resources

Technology does not just refer to the online environment. It also covers a very wide range of products, devices and everyday appliances, many of which offer opportunities for providing interesting and different ways to engage and enthuse learners and general members of the community. If you agree with the notion of offering up your school's physical infrastructure and resources to the local community, then this must extend to actual physical ICT devices as well as your online offerings. Remember, communities exist online in the same way that they exist through physical gatherings. Just like your students who are already engaging online in a range of communities, so the local people in your school's area are also likely to be engaging online and often through local connections. Drawing connections between these local physical and online communities through the school's digital footprint should be an aspiration for the school. In the same way we have talked about behaviour for online learning and assessment for online learning, so we are also extrapolating the idea to the concept of the *online* extended school.

The extended school is for your students as well as the community

While the notion of the extended school is very much about making the school part of the wider community, at the same time it is also about returning to the lesson design for your classroom-based students armed with the knowledge that the extended school not only exists but is of a high standard. Knowing that there are a range of extra learning opportunities for your students through the engagement of the extended school should influence your lesson planning on a range of levels.

You have to start with strong basic pedagogy: when designing an activity using technology to enhance the student learning experience, the first thing is to design it explicitly to be an active learning activity; the second is to ensure that the actual activity is student led; and the third thing is to ensure that it is not too large an activity: students can struggle to absorb the elements that make up a overly large activity and if it is too onerous (in terms of technicality, length, scope, etc.) the students will become bored and will disengage from the learning activity. If this happens, it is going to be very difficult to get them to re-engage with the activity or ICT should you attempt to use either again. Students are very situation experience-led, and a negative experience can create an almost insuperable barrier to their future engagement or participation. An unpleasant learning experience can create mind barriers to learners and, depending on the learner involved, if they were a peer leader for example, then their reluctance may be transmitted to their peers within the group. Keeping this in mind, the examples and ideas we present here for using ICT and media devices to enhance learning will try to model ways of avoiding these barriers.

Use the familiar whenever you can

Fundamentally, to engage students, you need to provide tangible context links. It is very difficult for students to conceptualise intangibles unless they are familiar with them. As a result, the ruling principle when engaging in enhanced learning requires either a familiar technology or a familiar context. Put simply: as much as is possible use technology that the students themselves use. The art or trick is to use the students' devices in a way that they themselves do not normally use them. Very rarely do students use their ICT in a structured and purposeful way, and it is this aspect that enables you as a teacher to use familiar technology to engage and inspire them.

The same might also be said of the local community – community members may also have access to ICT, but are not using it to the fullest extent or engaging with the notions of learning communities. The history department, for example, could run a community-focused project in which students and older members of the local community worked together to demonstrate how small mini-interviews, photographs and artefacts can all be easily digitally captured through a simple tablet or smartphone. The local community could be provided with a simple and easy-to-access space to store these artefacts online with the openly stated objective of the students using these digitally stored artefacts to practise and engage with as part of their lessons. Students are always delighted to show someone how to use basic technology, but in this case it is for a valid and helpful learning cause. That type of thinking in terms of projects would fulfil a range of ideas about the extended school and the *online* extended school.

What we are amalgamating here is the concept of ICT infrastructure, both online and physical devices, with the dual notions of flipped classrooms and the extended school. Remember, if you are unsure about how to extend learning beyond the classroom, then revisit the section on flipped classrooms in Chapter 2, which explores this notion of activities outside the classroom or sports field in greater detail.

Setting up a video project with the notion of the extended school

Consider the basic concept of how you might set up a video project as part of your teaching. This should not be a new concept: video cameras have been used in schools for a long time, and teachers and students should be using video cameras on a regular basis to capture their work and using this footage for reflection or evidence for assessment. In addition, students frequently capture images and video as part of their personal use of ICT. However, if we now start to think about some of the key concepts that we have explored in the book, we can develop the notion of the video project in a range of ways. First, let us revisit some of those key concepts briefly.

Let the students do the work

You want to be sure that your effort is focused around designing the learning opportunities, not on being a specialist in technology or doing all of the labour-intensive uploading or creating. Those tasks are opportunities for the students to learn and you need to allow students to extract the maximum learning from those activities.

Behaviour for online learning

You want to reinforce to students' safe practice that is not just respectful of ethics, but that also recognises the learning inherent within online activity that can be facilitated by community members functioning for one another.

Assessment for online learning

Students should be wholly familiar with the purpose and assessment requirements around which their online work is based. They should be looking to reflectively engage with their online work and generate as much high-quality formative feedback as possible as part of their online work, both as individuals and as groups.

The online extended school

Teachers and students should be looking to recognise how the school's digital footprint, both in terms of online offerings and physical media devices, can be utilised to help promote opportunities within the local community.

*****

Now that we have revisited those key concepts, we can consider how we might reshape our former notions of the video project to help meet those key aims.

Take any subject at random – let us suppose our hypothetical teacher is a science teacher who teaches all the sciences, but specialises in physics. One of the key aims of the school is to increase the numbers of girls who take physics beyond the school-leaving age, and it wants to deliver a short piece of the curriculum in such a way that all students, but particularly girls, are inspired and become fascinated with physics to the point at which they start to consider optional extended study.

The first step is to create a project space on the school's VLE, or through a commercial blogging website, where a range of text, photographs and video footage can be held and accessed only by a restricted group – namely the students and the teacher. In addition, they also create a project space that is accessible to the local community thus safeguarding the two separate areas to be safe and secure.

The next step would be to consider what the topic or theme might be – 'physics in the workplace' – would be a suitable title for the kind of project that takes students outside the classroom and inspires them to see how physics is used in industry.

Any further step would now be shaped by the input of the students and the wider local community. By setting out the framework for the video project to the students, our science teacher should then flip the classroom and set the students off researching what the project should look like. This will include communicating with the local community through their own networking via their parents. At every stage of the process, the science teacher would reinforce safe online practice, for example using parents to write to external members of the community on their behalf.

What our science teacher would be hoping for is a video project shaped by the students and the input from the local community. In particular, they could set out the theme of females in the workplace and ask students to ensure that this is properly represented and discussed through the lesson time before the students engage with online research and content gathering.

At all times, our science teacher would be putting into place opportunities for reflection, formative assessment and formative feedback. In addition, they would monitor the space online and initiate discussions in the classroom around the key behaviour for online learning principles and how these should be adhered to. Students could reflect on where their behaviour online had helped their own learning or that of others as part of the project.

In terms of the technical side of things, there are a range of apps or software that students could use to put the different footage together. Some students will be knowledgeable about this area – those who are more able in video editing. Thus our science teacher might ask the video editors for each group to draw up the success criteria for what a good app or piece of software looks like. They then might ask the directors of the group what their success criteria are. This constant engagement of the different students with the different aspects of their projects is central to assessment for learning, but it does not have to take place wholly in the classroom. The discussion might take place in the classroom, but then the individual student might append their interpretation into their group's project page. They could then receive formative feedback from their own group online on their own personal interpretation of the project. The role of the science teacher is to patrol these online discussions and perform the same role that they do in the physical classroom – that of the learned other. For example, they might ask challenging questions or they might ask for contributions from the more reluctant student members.

At the end of the project, those in the local community who have participated with the earlier stages will be interested to know how the project has evolved. The teacher could then make some of the content available online for members of the local community to review and engage with themselves. There might be a physical open evening where video footage is shown and visitors can meet and talk with the actual groups involved. There might also be a guest speaker from an adult female who talks about what it is like to be a female in an area of work dominated by men.

The end project should be of a very high quality with lots of opportunities for learning in a range of areas. The amount of lesson time involved could be really quite low in number. The flipped classroom concept pushes the work into the students' own time and also makes it the more engaging online aspect. The local community is involved and empowered through its engagement and the main aim of increasing the profile of women in physics achieved successfully. At all times, the students would be engaged, differentiated for and involved in a range of learning, both within their specific curriculum matter and also within wider, softer transferable skills such as collaboration, maturity and contextual knowledge of the workplace.

The extended school and the flipped classroom

We have previously touched on the concept of the flipped classroom (see Chapter 2), but here we are giving an idea of its practical use by thinking about the notion of the extended school from the student's perspective not just the local community. It is worth reminding ourselves that we are not following the conventional model of flipped classroom, which involves watching video lectures at home. Rather, we are taking the practical learning aspects normally done in the classroom and focusing on doing this on location in and around the school. To be really effective, and to achieve its full potential, the flipped classroom activity should be blended with cloud computing and communication-based software, which can then enable a coherent and inclusive learning environment. Using ICT in a creative and mobile way enables the flipped classroom to become an integral element of the enhanced learning experience for students. In particular, it provides ownership of the learning – a key tenet when trying to think about elements of learning that will inspire students.

Using mobile devices, as with any project or activity, requires purposeful briefing to ensure that students are clear about the elements of the activity and what they are attempting to achieve for each element. Remember that the central concept of behaviour for learning applies to the use of mobile technologies. For this conceptualised project, we are going to use a tablet computer with access to mobile broadband. This is becoming much more common as a standard feature on tablets, and the range of providers is increasing.

Citizenship, mobile technology and the extended school

The subject area that we are going to consider this time is citizenship. We are going to adapt a particular community and environmental activity that a secondary school in Hertford undertook annually. It focused on supporting the Hertford Countryside Management Service to reclaim areas of woodland and scrub. The school provides teams from all year groups for a weekend and under the direction of the management service clears and restores designated areas of woodland.

The context setting would be to identify local areas that have public access and that would benefit from community action. This could cover: clearing scrub, creating a garden area for disabled people, decorating a youth centre and so on – the options are endless. This is an activity that would allow groups of students to select an area that they believe would benefit from community action and create a five-minute short, a two-minute presentation and a leaflet to support their idea showing the benefits that it would bring to the community. The outcome from this would be a presentation of their idea to the local residents, local councillors and the local landowner.

The stages of this as a flipped project would be initially in the classroom, creating the working groups and developing some ideas and locations for improving the community. For each group's chosen area of focus, they could arrange an offsite visit, take notes, photos and videos and upload them to a shared area in a cloud-based area – either the school's VLE or within a selected commercially offered storage space. Back in the classroom, they are able to review and refine these to provide an agreed area and activity that will form the focus of their presentation.

The constant gathering, reflection and discussion of resources gathered through interaction then provides the point at which the next input occurs: planning the stages to create the presentation. They are then able to create their plan of action, which, because they are able to use their cloud storage and communication software, they can complete by planning and allocating who does what outside class time. At all times, the teacher will be reinforcing safe student practice and ensuring the students adhere to the school's behaviour for online learning ethics. The teacher is able to monitor the group's work online to ensure that progress is being made and that all the students are engaged in the group work and process such as compiling their leaflet and film or slide show. As always, lesson time can be for the group to come back into the classroom just for review, reflection and discussion as a physical group. This session would also offer teacher input, which would cover formative feedback on adding sound, commentary or music to their film or slide show and giving input about visual impact for a wide range of readers for the leaflet. This classroom session would result in a final film, interview, presentation, note collection and schedule ready for the final pre-production editing, dubbing and practice run-throughs. Their final videos or slideshows would be uploaded to the cloud and they would also upload their final version of their presentations. All of these would be available for monitoring by the teacher, but led by the individual groups. At the end of the project, the groups are able to present their ideas to the rest of the class and constructive feedback is given for final adjustments before their presentation to their target group representatives.

This type of project, wholly focused on students' learning, but within the context of the extended school, is clearly raising the profile and engagement for all students of the subject area of citizenship and would inspire all involved to develop this subject area even further in their own time.

Acquiring the media devices

None of the devices outlined in this chapter need be expensive. This is deliberate, as the use of ICT to enhance student learning requires that all the students take part and not just a select few. This does not remove the issue that it is challenging for schools to ensure all their students have access to media devices that could enhance their learning opportunities.

There are a number of possible routes that an individual teacher (or indeed the school) might pursue. First, an appeal to parents might be in order. It is not uncommon for schools to advise parents as to which devices it would be useful for their children to have. If a school library is being innovative with ebooks, then they should ensure parents know that an ebook reader or an app for ebooks on a tablet will enable students to tap into this innovation. A second route might be through the governing body as this has access to a number of sources of innovation and sometimes has a separate fund for such initiatives. The main approach currently being explored by schools that have adopted tablets-for-all types of policy is for the school's ICT budget to be wholly rethought in terms of structure so that devices can be bought at a zero increase in net cost. Many schools are reshaping their ICT budgets and moving away from buying and maintaining rooms full of desktop PCs. Instead, they are reducing the desktop numbers to fewer, more specialised desktops – such as for media or art – and redeploying the money on mobile devices such as tablets.

To increase your chances of success when you are looking for extra funding, think about who you could choose to approach for extra funding. For example, local businesses are always keen to be part of the extended school, particularly if the school is embracing the concept of extended school and working hard to support local communities including local businesses. Undertake some good research in advance and you might find that if the project is one that fits in a company's areas of interest then it will be more likely to support your request of a donation of equipment.

The smartphone as part of the extended school

Name: Anonymous
School: Secondary school
Age phase: 11–18
Your role: Modern foreign languages teacher.
Types of technology: Smartphone.

Why you/the school introduced it: we were trying to engage the students with an awareness of the local community and its needs so that it contextualised what we were trying to do in the classroom with their learning.

What was introduced and how?: We used the smartphone to enhance student's use of French and Spanish. The students discussed, as part of their lesson, the town's high street and how useful it would be to have an information slide show of the town centre in the tourist information office which allowed French and

Spanish speakers to be able to find out about the town centre in their own language. From this discussion, the students were set homework over the weekend, which required taking ten photographs of their local high street showing the diversity of shops and businesses in existence. Back at school, the teacher, in one of the IT classrooms, showed the students how to use Windows Moviemaker by demonstrating with a set of photographs taken on their own mobile phone. They showed them how to get the photos off their phones onto the application and create a three-minute long slide show including a title page and credits. Some of the students used apps on their smartphones that they had used before. The students then created their individual slide shows, which they saved.

For the next part of the project, the teacher then split the students into pairs. Then, using their slide show for modelling, they demonstrated how they could put a commentary in French or Spanish into the slideshow so that it matched each slide. The paired students then decided which of their slide shows they wanted to use and which language they would provide the commentary in. One of the pair would write and record the commentary and the other would compose and insert subtitles which matched both the commentary and the slides. This took the second lesson to complete. The third lesson enabled the students to complete their slide show, whereon they uploaded the finished product to an area that could be accessed by the local community. In addition, they then played their slide show to the whole class and reflected on the end project and how much they had learned from undertaking this activity.

What problems or successes did you meet?: The evaluation by both students and teacher demonstrated that the level of engagement and learning was much higher that they had expected.

What are the next steps?: Some of the students went on to add further slide shows to the public area, but as part of their own work rather than as part of the structured school project. This was because they were of Italian heritage and liked the idea of having Italian slide shows as well as French and Spanish on the public area.

CHAPTER

8

Embedding ICT in practice

Chapter summary

Build on good pedagogy
Harness the knowledge of your students rather than fear it
Planning to use technology
Making a lesson with technology successful
Core strategies for making a lesson with technology a success
Technology that could be used as part of whole-school practice

Build on good pedagogy

Embedding the use of ICT into your teaching practice does not mean that you have to change the way you have always taught. Throughout this book, we have stressed you must carry on with the sound principles that underpin your pedagogy. Where in your normal teaching you ensure all learning experiences are undertaken by the students – they read out the play, they work out the equations, they undertake the experiment – so you do the same with technology. Let the students do the work!

Where you adopt good behaviour-for-learning principles, so you do the same with technology: adapting it into either behaviour for online learning or behaviour for learning with technology. Even assessment for learning gets the same treatment. It becomes assessment for online learning or assessment for learning with technology. If you hold onto these principles then you can ensure that strong learning will take place when you teach using ICT. However, there is a stronger and more positive effect to be had from bringing good ICT pedagogy into your teaching. Your students are going to be safer in their own *personal* use of technology as a direct result of your teaching. They are going to be thinking about learning opportunities when they are posting on their social networking sites. They are going to be taking your strong pedagogy and infusing it into their use of technology in their own time.

Technology in teaching is not a new thing. Computers, devices and interactive whiteboards have been around for a long time already so it does not necessarily mean that you have to change the way you already use ICT throughout your lessons and teaching. You may already be building on a basis of good practice. If you already use ICT in your teaching then there is a good chance you do so because you believe that using ICT in your lessons creates a chance that ICT will enhance your students' learning experiences and, by implication, enhance your own practice.

Harness the knowledge of your students rather than fear it

One of the things that deters teachers from using ICT to enhance students' learning is the fear or belief that the students, or some of the students at least, know more than you. Rest assured that students know only limited amounts, generally learned by trial and error, and they will not know how to maximise their learning through better use of this knowledge. Already, you will begin to see that your ability to see learning opportunities is what marks you out as a teacher. Specific technological knowledge is not essential for you to point, ask a challenging question and for the student to then develop their learning of a topic further through both *their* knowledge of technology and *your* knowledge of learning. Teaching is not a craft: teaching is an academic subject centred around pedagogy, and that is why you are the learned other in the classroom or on the sports field, regardless of the premise that some of your students might have more specific technological knowledge than you in a very narrow field. For you to assuage your fears and be accepted by the students as knowledgeable, it is important that whenever you use technology to enhance student learning you also focus on not trying to be the font of all knowledge. Rather, you are going to demonstrate to the students that your evaluation and decision-making skills are the things that they should be seeking out in you.

Planning to use technology

The purpose of this next section is to give you some guidance on ways to approach both planning to use ICT and delivering it in the classroom. Good practice is a set of procedures, more than anything, that enables someone to produce a consistent and expected outcome. What follows are some core guidelines that underpin the training of ICT and computer science classroom teaching practice. Remember, just as every teacher is an 'English teacher', so we are all 'ICT teachers'. ICT, as we know it, is no longer the preserve of specialist teachers. It has become mainstream and we are all responsible for showing our students how to improve their learning and understanding through using ICT effectively and safely.

The first notion to discard is that ICT is there to enhance your teaching practice. The purpose of using ICT is to enhance student learning. If it does that, then, by extension, it will enhance your practice. If using ICT does not enhance their learning then be prepared to go back to what you were doing before. Like most good experiences, using ICT to enhance the learning experience does not just happen. It takes purpose and planning: the more you do it, the easier it becomes; just like teaching your own subject and just like in your own subject specialism. So, the first thing is to plan what you want the students to learn and then to work out how you and your use of ICT could potentially help them to learn it.

Much of the use of ICT for enhanced learning is likely to require access to ICT devices – either mobile or fixed. It will depend on what school you are in and what access your students have to ICT. This might vary from being in a school in which every student has a tablet to one in which the students and you have to arrange to visit an ICT suite as part of a booked programme of access. Whatever the case, there are some core areas of strategy that make the difference between an effective teaching and learning experience and a poor experience in the classroom.

Making a lesson with technology successful

Teaching in a classroom, or even on a sports field, where the students have access to technology can be challenging. These devices or fixed desktop PCs are points of interaction and hold all the temporary long-term memory that the students access at will through a search engine. This means there is another type of learned other in the lesson other than you – and it is in electronic form. It is better that you appreciate that these are the challenges that face a teacher who teaches students who have access to technology, and understand that you need to control the situation with patience and understanding rather than frustration; and indeed it would be foolhardy for you to attempt to compete with the technology for the status of learned other. Remember some of our central tenets around behaviour for learning with ICT as well as the notion that not all students are technophiles or indeed technophobes. Just as you need to differentiate for the different student abilities in your classroom, so you also need to differentiate for the students' differing levels of knowledge and enthusiasm around ICT. Just as the student with literacy problems will try to hide this weakness behind inappropriate behaviour, so too will the student who cannot demonstrate competence of ICT in front of their peers. Having this mindset before you even begin planning the lesson, as well as during the delivery of the lesson, will ensure that these students are catered for and their abilities are used productively in the lesson. There are also some issues that run across all learners, and we have tried to set out some useful core strategies for making any lesson where the students have access to technology in the form of ICT equipment a success.

Core strategies for making a lesson with technology a success

The following section contains a series of strategies that you should be incorporating into your lesson planning and delivery. Having technology in the classroom or on the sports field means you must make adaptations to your pedagogy as technology naturally enthuses but, at the same time, it does present an extra challenge for both you and your students. These adaptations will enable you to deliver successful lessons and avoid the pitfalls of the inexperienced teacher. They range from the start of the lesson where you are briefing the students in the classroom and the giving of instructions around the usage of technology to the way you move around the classroom.

Briefing in the classroom

This section of the lesson imposes a range of structures to the lesson and to the equipment to ensure the students are engaged safely and productively in the activities that you have planned. It should take no more than ten minutes from the start to releasing them for the task. You should aim to bring the students away from their technology and bring them to the front of the classroom. Here, you are able to explain the activities that you want them to undertake with technology as part of the lesson using the following guidelines:

- Establish a solid groundwork of esafety practice.
- Set out the principles of behaviour for learning with ICT.
- Establish how assessment for learning with ICT will be taking place.
- Explain, model and scaffold the task or activity and check the understanding of all the students of the task or activity they are to engage in.
- Set out a structure in terms of time and the length of the different tasks in the lesson.
- Establish success criteria for the selection and use of temporary technology in the form of apps, software or information retrieval.

Instructions in the main part of the lesson

This is used for refocusing and re-establishing expectations of the students as they are working. You should build some key stop points into the lessons to be able to deliver and redeliver instructions in the main lesson. Your rationale for stopping the class should be that either the students are not approaching the task in the way you require and need refocusing or that you have deliberately scheduled a transition in activity that will require further modelling.

If you find that the technology is distracting to your instructions and modelling, be quite firm in how you direct the students to focus on you and not the technology – they will struggle to switch off from interacting with technology and one another to be wholly compliant and focused on your instruction again. Adopt a four-point strategy:

- Students must switch off their monitors or technology screens temporarily.
- Students must be silent.
- Students must face you and not focus on one another or the technology.
- Students will demonstrate their understanding through question and answer.

You must approach this as a consistent procedure every time so that the students become conditioned into good behaviour for learning with technology. At all times, reinforce that the behaviour they demonstrate should be conducive not just to their own learning but to that of their peers as well.

Moving around in a classroom with ICT equipment

It is our experience that many teachers can be quite static when faced with a room full of students all focused on technology. They will often stay very close to the board or the teacher's desk. The reason for this is that they do not see themselves as having specialist ICT knowledge. However, if you consider some of the key concepts we have explored in the book, you will recall that we have said you should not be the one with the specialist knowledge. Instead, you are the specialist at evaluation and decision making. If the student needs to learn how to do something, then they will just pull up a tutorial on YouTube and self-learn that knowledge and skill temporarily. Instead, your role is to make suggestions or ask challenging questions that necessitate the student to rethink the quality of the work and the way they are using ICT to learn or present their work. In the lesson, you should set out the objective of operating all over Bloom's taxonomy with confidence and skill. With you operating as a learned other, the students are going to be challenged to learn and process their knowledge and skills with more precision and sophistication.

At a fundamental level, just as in any subject, circulation is essential if you are going to be promoting good assessment for learning principles. You cannot offer feedback if you do not circulate. You cannot use proximity as a method of behavioural control if you are not circulating effectively. You cannot dictate the pace of the lesson and control transitions without the formative assessment knowledge informed by circulation. That extra information about how your students are progressing then gives you the information about whether an additional briefing or instruction is necessary, particularly if a number of students are having a common point of difficulty. At all times, think about the idea of problem solving and encourage the students to collaborate and confer about how they are problem solving, what technology they are using and what their success criteria are for their choice of problem-solving method.

Technology that could be used as part of whole-school practice

In the examples that follow, any implications for software will be explained as required. Where they are visual activities using media then the software, as much as possible, will be that which is freely and generally available such as Windows Movie Maker. Using freely accessible software is important as it will offer a student the opportunity to work on their projects outside of school, an outcome that underpins the flipped classroom model. (Note that some of the media described in the following section may be familiar to you and some may not.)

However, the purpose of the media and how it is used in your lessons is to provide a *familiar context* for the media and the activity – your students will likely already have some familiarity of experience with ICT and media devices. Remember, the more familiar or engaging that the students find the activity context, the more willing they are likely to be experimenting with the technology. Building in contexts that draw on the local environment will also increase not just the familiar, but the potential connections that can be drawn between your class-based work and opportunities for the local community to engage with your project and experience learning opportunities of their own, as well as enhance the outcomes of your students.

Beyond the basic devices of desktop PC, laptop, tablet, smartphone and ebook reader, you should be thinking about what devices are actually used in the workplace or as part of further study at a higher level. To help you, we have listed some interesting devices that you might not have thought of using in your lessons. The range of devices described here is not exhaustive, but they are ones that we have actually used to develop activities for non-ICT specialists to be able to incorporate into their own subject areas. We are not necessarily recommending any particular manufacturers as both technology and software vary in terms of how useful it is depending on the task and time of year. At any point in its life, a device or software may well slip out of mainstream usage and others will become popular. We have tried to focus on a more eclectic range of media while recognising the place of mainstream devices such as laptops and tablets in the scheme of things. The key thing for you to consider is whether any of them make you rethink your ideas about ICT and devices in the classroom.

Headcam or digi-cam

It is becoming more common for people to use small camcorders that fit on the head. Certainly camcorders are becoming more popular with cyclists and, in particular, with the parents of students who cycle. It is reported more frequently in television programmes that headcams are being adopted by commuters who cycle. Other uses often seen on television documentaries are the use of headcams by potholers and underground rescue teams. These offer quite an exciting and engaging background for introducing a project activity that uses headcams as the means of recording.

Thinking laterally about this concept of headcams to create activities means you can offer opportunities for headcams to be used in a creative way to engage and enhance learning for students of all ages. From geography to art, from dance to drama, headcams could give students an innovative and different viewpoint as well as turn a mundane activity into one that is exciting and interesting. What can a rugby flanker see when he runs down the wing? What decision making can he make with that field of vision? You can immediately see how any teacher could enliven opportunities for reflection using point-of-view footage from a headcam.

There are two activities that this device is very well suited to. The first can be classroom based and the second 'field based': the first use could be for a science (biology), design technology or English subject activity. Here the digi-cam is worn in class and a normal lesson is delivered. The digi-cam might be worn for the whole lesson or just part of it; this is entirely the choice of you, the teacher. The essence of this activity is that when the video is played back it will show exactly how students move and look around during a lesson. Apart from providing a context for gaze, physical movement or attention points, it would be a very useful activity feedback for the teacher. The analysis might look at how long the students concentrate on the 'task in hand' before they become bored or distracted. This feedback activity could be constructed as paired or groups. As a whole-class activity, it may tend to become too fraught as not all students will be able to be engaged, whereas pairs and small groups do enable this engagement. An interesting outcome of this as an activity will be the degree of head movement rather than just eye movement that takes place, and even the students will be surprised by how much there is. How will this analysis take place? The video can be directly downloaded to a computer and played back via a projector, so no editing of specialist skills are necessary. Knowing what you want them to do means that you give them an analysis framework table that can be filled in as they watch the playback. What is an outcome? Suggestions for strategies that will keep them more focused. How will this add to learning? Well, apart from the students' surprise at the degree and frequency of movement, the analysis and recommendations develop structured thinking skills, which will impact on embedded learning skills.

The second, as a field-based activity, centres on observation. Again this will have application to the previous subject areas but could, depending on the focus, include any other subjects taught in the school. One such activity might involve developing an activity that requires the students to take a focused walk with the digi-cam and to go and look at a local church and find six facts about the church, exploring these on the digi-cam video. They then write a five-line explanation about each of the facts shown on the digi-cam. As a further activity, the video could be downloaded to Windows Movie Maker, for example, and then the students can read their written facts as a narration to match the video that they shot. If you were teaching a modern languages lesson, the narration could be in French, for example. This could be taken further by putting subtitles in English to match the video and the narration. From a science – biology (botany) or geography – activity, the students could follow a watercourse, particularly of a stream, from where it starts to where it meets a larger stream or river. This as a record of how a stream develops becomes an enhanced experience. From the botany point of view, filming the changes in vegetation as the stream matures would provide a specific focus.

In-car cam

This is another piece of technology that is gaining popularity, especially through the growth in lifelogging. It is a small high definition (HD) camcorder that is placed on the inside of the car windscreen, recording events as you drive along. You might be wondering where this fits into education, but the proliferation of in-car camcorders has made available a rich range of evidence. For example, the Chelyabinsk meteor that exploded over Russia in 2013 was captured on thousands of in-car camcorders. From this footage, mathematicians were able to work out speed, entry and a whole range of fascinating statistics. Imagine if this were your own A-level maths or physics class. Using the meteor as an example, you could get them to develop similar mathematical models from other footage or data.

Thinking like this means the in-car cam offers a range of opportunities, for example the Industrial Revolution of 1850–1900 as a history topic. The students would be able to use video footage collated by others to identify both types and the location of industrial activity passed during the journey and create an audio-visual project from it. Using their own imagery brings the experience and the learning to life and starts to make them think about how they are constantly lifelogging information and how this information can be shared.

Journeys that are captured could be focused in a different way so that the footage is evaluated for how it addresses environmental awareness. It could centre round their journey to school and could stimulate discussions about impact or alternatives. This then could actually make citizenship, for example, interesting and explicitly relevant to the students.

Digital voice recorder

Digital voice recorders are portable high-quality audio devices and are far removed from the dictaphones of old. They are of a higher quality and have a longer recording capacity than that available on a mobile phone. As a result, they can be used as a project activity in their own right or can contribute to extending and enhancing another activity.

Of course, one obvious use of digital voice recorders is to get students to interview people, and certainly they are an excellent device for being able to record history. There are several people still living who experienced World War I, and the same is also true for World War II veterans. Voice recorders offer students opportunities for collecting 'living memories' and to upload them to a shared online area ready for analysis and reflection. The world wars were not just about the fighting and the politics. What was called the 'home front' is a rich source of what it was actually like. While students might not have relatives still alive from either conflict, certainly by arranging to visit care and nursing homes in which many of the people who lived through the wars now live themselves is an excellent environment in which to capture this living history. Certainly both the care homes and the residents are delighted to meet and talk with students today and share their memories. Using a digital voice recorder and some on the other devices described would be perfect for such a project. Is it just history? What about the focus being how the local environment (houses, roads, leisure and the workplace) has changed between the two wars?

All of these suggestions offer enhanced learning opportunities and sharing projects that the normal curriculum tends to ignore. The planning really is making the arrangements to visit and deciding what questions to ask and this second part can form part of the class preparation: deciding as a class the questions to ask, why they are valid, what should the students 'do' with the answers they receive, how might there be shared? After all, not all learning has to be driven by examinations or targets.

(Even if you do not have access to more professional digital voice recorders, there will be an app on a smartphone that enables students to record and upload their findings.)

Decibel (noise) meter

When considering media devices, it is important that you look to industry for real-life examples of devices in the field. Some of these devices require considerable engagement and understanding in a specialist field and can re-present a subject in a new and innovative light. The decibel meter device measures and captures noise levels and presents this information using a range of charts and numbers as part of the accompanying software. It can be connected to a computer and capture the noise data as it happens, either as a picture trace or data which can be saved in a spreadsheet and analysed later on the computer. This offers opportunities for group as well as individual activities and a range of contexts in which the data can be applied. The classroom itself offers possibilities for looking into and investigating the way sound affects the teaching and learning environment by considering the layout, size and equipment within it. It may be fair to suggest that the maximum range of opportunities presented for the sound meter are outside the classroom, but if you consider local building applications and regulations and the local council's work, then the noise meter could be an interesting recontextualisation of an everyday subject. This might include comparing types of 'industrial activity' – is a construction site noisier to the passer-by than road repairs are? How are these things measured against time spans? Is a relatively short, loud noise such as an aircraft taking off and passing overhead more or less distracting that a construction site on which machinery is in constant use?

The smartphone

While this might not quite fit into the normal interpretation of ICT to enhance student learning, we are including it in this list as the smartphone is both one of the least acceptable devices for use in schools and, at the same time, one of the most engaging devices for many students. It is sense, therefore, to determine ways in which it can be used effectively. Its biggest selling point for a teacher is that it can be all things – it can be a camera, a word processor, an MP3 recorder, a rhyming dictionary and so forth. Even further, once an app has been designed, the smartphone can be something we do not have at the moment. In other words, the smartphone is capable of being retrofitted – fitted with a new technology.

chapter 8 Embedding ICT in practice

Most students have mobile phones and many have smartphones. The majority of schools ban or restrict use of any phones, but used in a purposeful manner they can be a great learning resource because students are familiar with them. Students tend not to use them in a structured manner, and there are a range of features in even the more basic phones that provide an engaging feature for a learning activity. Almost all mobile phones have a built-in camera and most are able to film video. For the latter, they are somewhat limited due to memory capacity, and it may be argued that using a mobile phone for filming is not good educational practice. However, in many cases, it is purely the fact that students have not been shown how to use devices in a structured way, embedding good practice, that they engage in low learning behaviour on their smartphones – remember our mantra of behaviour for online learning. This applies to how students use their smartphones in particular.

Certainly an early stage at which mobile phones can be used to enhance learning is to undertake a class audit of the facilities available on their phones, determine who uses which feature and what they use it for. By conducting an audit activity, students will be motivated and enabled to extend their knowledge and understanding of how smartphones can be used in a project format. From this point, activities can be developed that engage the student and can be used to enhance their learning experience. By using smartphones in a creative, structured and purposeful way, students can be shown and taught how they can really enhance their learning experiences both as part of their school day and in their own personal use.

A very simple and engaging flipped classroom activity is to set the students a homework task of taking five photographs about a particular topic or subject on their smartphones – something that many students will find engaging and interesting. They can then go on to produce a five-slide slideshow using the photographs and then record a commentary to go with them. This is easily achieved using, for example, one of the many free editing apps on their smartphones or tablets or they can transfer the footage to a desktop PC and use the free Windows Movie Maker program. The next point is to upload them to the school's cloud area or simply bring them in and present them in the classroom for discussion. Thus, even if your school is unhappy about the students using their smartphones in the lesson, you can still easily use them to engage the students in a range of activities that affect the learning that goes on inside the classroom.

Name: Richard Broad
School: Lampton School
Age phase: 11–16
Your role: English teacher.
Types of technology: Interactive whiteboard.

Why you/the school introduced it: I needed to get the students to understand how the bigger picture worked in poetry. One of the key things I wanted to develop was a record of the class work as they deconstructed associated art images alongside the poetry, ready for further reflection at a later date. The IWB enabled both images and poetry to be displayed, annotated, stored, exported and shared and then later reflected on with ideas being built up and refined.

What was introduced and how?: I used pictures embedded into the IWB to teach the themes of the GCSE poetry we were covering. For example, I would ask pupils to give me the story behind *The Awakening Conscience* by William Holman Hunt before we start looking at Hardy's *The Ruined Maid* – from this, I could direct questions about the themes/ideas/values/attitudes apparent in the picture from the artist's perspective and from the students' perspective as viewers before approaching the poetry. Often, these pictures are in some way linked, so I might have pictures up with the pyramids and the Olympic Games and ask the pupils how they are connected. This is something I introduced to the school and it works particularly well with IWB as the pictures can be annotated for the 'precise details' they would be expected to pick out in the poem.

What problems or successes did you meet?: Sometimes the pupils, depending on ability, do need a little more direction and the questions you pose need to be less open, but other than that it is a good way to get them thinking of the 'bigger picture' and making the links they need for the AQA GCSE poetry across time exam.

What are the next steps?: I need to allow the students to get used to saying what they think. They need to be allowed to practise/discuss in groups as, if the IWB is used regularly, then their responses do become more analytical and the conversation more in depth due to the fact that they record their reflections and come back to them for refinement and challenge at a later date.

CHAPTER

Conclusion

ICT, or technology, changes at an ever increasing speed. The main players today – Google, Facebook, Apple, Samsung and Microsoft – are all rapidly investing in very new start-up companies or any app or company that makes an instant success. An example of this would be Facebook's purchase of Whatsapp in February 2014 for $19billion. The main thrust of these purchases is centred around data. From fitness trackers to shopping online, these companies are looking to see how they can increase their presence in the way society uses data as part of their daily lives. Young people are at the forefront of this rapid progress as they are often the first adopters of new technology. When they have finished with their latest smartphone, they will upcycle it to their parents thus ensuring that all members of the households are updating their technology on a sequential basis. The companies are aware of this and phase out support for devices and software to ensure there is a time limit to the life of a tablet or smartphone – this is known as built-in obsolescence. Thus, in a very short space of time, tablets and smartphones have become ubiquitous in the modern household. Fast broadband speeds, both fixed and mobile, are now widespread and have also become quite standard. This makes a big difference as users can satisfy all their requirements whether at a sitting desk or on the move. The main reason for maintaining fixed desktop pieces of technology in schools was that they had access to fast internet as well as being powerful pieces of technology. With mobile broadband and fast wi-fi, the mobile device is able to compete with the fixed desktop equipment and move the 'office' into the mobile world of the user. We can see–with these main pieces of technology and internet up to speed and power–that all the required components for the next stage of this technological society are in place. All of this places an intense focus on the interaction between individuals and groups and how data move around between them all. This large amount of data being generated through activities such as lifelogging is expanding exponentially, and yet schools and governments are struggling to deal with this historical moment of change.

In many ways, schools form an immensely traditional medium – many are still using the tools of the 19th-century era of paper, pens, exercise books, paper mark books and paper exams conducted within examination halls. Yet, when you step outside the school buildings and you see young people clustered around tablets and smartphones, interacting in groups and online, you can quickly see that this is what the future will look like for education. This contrast is further placed under pressure by higher education's adoption of modern technology, collaborative work

chapter 9 Conclusion

and assessment, eportfolios, VLEs and custom-designed apps and software for their students. This has resulted in significant transition issues for students moving from one phase of education to the next. To be fair, some schools are early adopters and have tried out the idea of issuing tablets to all children, placing learning online and experimenting with the concept of the classroom and the timetable. Some examination systems are slowly, torturously, in fact, moving into the online medium. Much of the issue is that some governments inspect and judge schools based on the examination system. Hence, instead of being something that flexes with progress and adapts itself to the learner, the examination system is slow moving and beholden to the past. Each student has to be assessed in an identical way to that of another student for this to happen. However, with collaborative online learning it is very difficult to assess individual contributions, and thus it falls out of favour with those seeking to demonstrate that their educational institution is meeting the demands of their government. In addition, technology is changing rapidly where educational systems do not. There needs to be a perspective from the educational establishment that embraces this rapid change and obsolescence. This educational perspective should then seek to design pedagogy that can withstand the disruption from the fast-moving technology medium.

The teacher who seeks to harmonise these two forces has a challenging job. They must satisfy their government's data-driven desire for individual assessment-based evidence of learning and progress and, at the same time, inspire their students to use collaborative technology to help progress their learning *and that of others*. If that were not challenging enough, technology changes at a bewildering speed. What is up and in vogue one minute is down and out the next. What is the best app one day is rapidly superseded the next. Having an approach to teaching that relies not on the teacher *knowing* the best apps and technology, but in getting the students to engage with their technology in a way that enhances their learning was always going to be the key strategy.

The strategies set out in this book started on a bedrock of good pedagogy. Students already construct their learning in the classroom instead of looking for the teacher to be the font of all knowledge. If the student does the work then the student does the learning. Our mantra at all times thus was: let the students do the work. In this way, they are availing themselves of opportunities to learn. In addition, we took solid approaches to learning, such as behaviour for learning and assessment for learning, and adapted them to the online collaborative communities that students find themselves in. Finally, we infused a strong sense of cybersafety throughout our work. Just as schools teach students to be safe in the real world, so schools need to teach students to be safe in the online world.

The end result has been a book that will not go out of date as soon as the next new technology company or app comes along. It contains advice that any teacher, regardless of their lack or otherwise of technological knowledge, can follow and use to inspire their students. These students, many of whom struggle with the traditional learning tools they are compelled to use in schools, will appreciate your enlightenment and reward you with enthusiasm and energy as well as a renewed passion for your own subject area. This is the main aim of the book – to inspire students to love learning and to love a subject in the way we have all learned to do.

We hope you have enjoyed this book and that your students are suitably inspired by your ability to bring ICT into their learning in a way they have not encountered before.

Index

access rights 28
Amazon 12
Android 11, 33, 61
anger management 59
animation 2
app communities 50
Apple 11, 12, 32, 33, 78, 105
apps 3–6, 11, 14, 19, 31–4, 37, 40, 57, 58, 59, 61, 62, 68, 77, 88, 91, 92, 96, 101, 106; choice of 32; data-storing 49; editing 102; Kindle 35, 68; notebook-style 37; running 6; social networking 46, 48, 49; third-party 14; and types of data 38; weather 32
art 102–3
artefact-building 23–4
assessment 18, 38, 47, 51, 71, 96, 106; controlled 71; formative 21, 97; for learning (AfL) 9, 21, 25, 27, 52; online 27, 48; paper-based 48; peer-to-peer 21, 76
autism 7, 9
Awakening Conscience, The 103

banking 62, 63
BBM codes 58
birdwatching 50
BlackBerry 32, 58, 61
blended learning 17–29; strategy for 20, 27
blogging 78
bluetoothing 4
book reviews 2
books 2, 8, 35, 40, 41, 68
boys 7, 35, 69
broadband 105
bullying 9 *see also* cyberbullying
BYOC 11
BYOD 11–12, 69; policy on 60–2; and security 60–2
BYOL 11
BYOPC 11
BYOT 11, 28, 33, 61–2

camcorders 13, 98
cameras 13, 74; digital 13; mini-37
chatrooms 59, 82
Chelyabinsk meteor 100
citizenship 89–90, 100
classroom discussion 27
cloud computing 11, 12, 18, 27–8, 37, 78, 89
cloud storage 12–13, 28, 58, 90; private 12–13, 79; public 12, 79
codes of conduct 64–7
community action 90
computer science 3, 68
copyright 35, 62
core knowledge/skills 5
creative thinking 3
creative writing 42
crowdsourced resources 60–1
cultural capital 45
curriculum 41, 52, 61, 62, 69, 80; marketisation of 41; personalising of 41–2
cyberbullying 9, 56–60, 62, 78; and education 59; low-level 59; responses to 57–8; and retaliation 58; and secure records 59; viral speed of 57
cybercriminals 62
cybersafety 62–3, 78, 106; training in 56, 59
cybersecurity 56, 59, 63–4, 81
cycling 98

decibel (noise) meters 101
digicams 99
digital citizenship 62
digital footprint 9, 75, 85, 87
digital voice recorders 100–1
dopamine 1
drag and drop 13
drama 24
dysgraphia 23, 37
dyslexia 9, 23
dyspraxia 23, 37

Index

ebook readers 2, 3, 31, 35, 98
ebooks 91; interactive 2
editing rights 28
Edmodo 53
email 12, 32, 44, 59, 62, 63, 64
endorphins 1
English as an additional language (EAL) 7, 23, 46, 68
eportfolios 28, 46, 71–4, 78, 106
esafety 36, 69, 96
ethics 64–7, 78; health and safety 66; location 65, 67; participation 65–6, 67; privacy 66; risk assessment 66, 67
examination system 106
extended school, the 9, 83
external hard drives 13
external memory 13

Facebook 2, 44–6, 49, 50, 56–8, 75, 105; 'school' 53
feedback 41, 44, 47, 53, 99; formative 25–6, 27, 47, 52; summative 27
Fetcheveryone.com 49
film 3, 13, 55
flash drives 13
FlickR 58
flipped classroom 17–18, 21, 38, 62, 64, 79, 88, 89, 90, 102
4G 14
frapes 57
further education 33–4

gaming 49
Gantt charts 38
girls 7
gmail 12, 62
Google 4–5, 11, 32, 33, 61, 78, 105
Google Docs© 12, 24, 28, 78
Google Drive 12
Google glass 4
GPS tracking/data 3, 49, 51
guide dogs 7

hacking 62, 63
hardware 3, 34, 37, 61
Hardy, Thomas 103
'Harnessing Technology' 74
HD cards 13
headcams 98–9
Hertford Countryside Management Service 89–90
higher education 33–4, 67, 72–3, 105–6

history, living 100
homework 17, 21–2, 38, 44–5, 47, 53, 75, 82, 92; models of 20
Hotmail 62

iCloud© 12, 78
Image Transfer 13
in-apps purchasing 36
in-car cam 99–100
Industrial Revolution 100
information and communication technology (ICT) 2–11, 17, 22, 37, 49, 52, 57–8, 60–3, 67–9, 89, 90, 98, 105, 107; administration of 26; changes in 105; and computers 10; cost of 91; and learning structure 18–21, 96; obsolescence of 34, 75, 105, 106; planning to use 94–5; purchasing of 34, 44; school-wide approach to 28; and student safety 9, 33, 34, 36, 47, 50–1, 55–9, 61; terminology of 11–15; and time management 48; updating of 34; user friendliness of 26, 77; whole-school approach to 67–9 *see also* mobile technologies
information management 56
inspiring students 1, 3, 107; through technology 7–10, 20, 49, 56, 71
Instagram 75
Instant Messenger (IM) 58, 63
interactivity 2, 3, 19, 24, 34, 43–6, 55, 59, 66, 96, 105
internet 12, 14–15, 32, 42, 75, 78, 79, 105; long-term memory of 39; speed of 14, 105
interviews 100
iOS 11
iPad minis 33, 36
iPads 4, 31, 33, 36, 61
iPhones 5, 31, 32, 33, 61
It's Learning 68, 72, 82

JavaScript 63, 68

keyboards, bluetoothed 37
Kindle Fire HD 35
Kindles 4, 8, 31, 35
knowledge 1–5, 9, 10, 19, 22–4, 32; access to 39; content 25; nature of 5, 39; storage of 5; temporary 6

la grande permission 1
law 62

learned others 76
learners 6–10, 18, 22, 23, 28, 29, 33, 34, 45, 46, 49, 50, 60, 80, 85, 86, 95, 106; diversity of 7; types of 8–9
learning 1, 2, 4–6, 9, 12, 43, 47, 69, 71, 73, 75, 91–4, 99; active 17; alternative 80–1; assessment for (AfL) 9, 21, 25, 27, 76, 93; distance 80; enhanced 20, 38, 93–5, 101; extended 18, 22; group 48; 'hidden' 45; interactive 49; location of 18; ownership of 89; physical 17; poor 48, 81; reflection on 74 *see also* online learning
learning community, the 22, 80
learning styles 27, 42
lifelogging 49–51, 99, 100, 105; and artefacts 51; and statistics 49, 51–2
logins 26, 56, 63, 75

malware 60, 61, 64
management of coursework/classwork 71–2
massive online open courses (MOOCs) 81
mathematics 41, 68
memory (of students) long-term 5, 38, 39; short-term 38
memory cards 13
memory sticks, USB 13, 14, 28
meritocracy 7
microcards 13
Microsoft 11, 12, 78, 105
Microsoft Office 2013 12, 34, 37
Microsoft Windows 13, 42
Microsoft Word 5, 39, 42
mindmapping 37–8
mobile phones 13, 14, 31, 57, 58, 68, 102
mobile technologies 3–4, 11, 31, 36–42, 48, 60, 78, 89, 95; access to 34, 38; availability of 34; banning of 4, 33, 34; cases for 36; competition in 33; and convergence 37; damage to 28, 36, 61, 69; investment in 36, 91; school policy on 36; sharing of 36; tipping point of 31 *see also* information and communication technology (ICT)
Moodle 72, 79
music 13, 14, 19, 72, 80, 90
My Pictures 13

netbooks 11
noise 101

online chat 49
online collaboration 22, 27, 47, 106

online group work 23–4, 27, 82; roles in 23, 76; tracking of 27
online identity 49, 58, 64
online learning 9, 12, 17, 22, 46, 49, 52, 72, 76, 80–1, 93, 106; behaviour for 9, 22, 46–8, 56, 89, 93, 96–7
online material 19, 23
online project space 24–6, 29, 51, 75–7, 82, 92
online resource management 28
online tutorials 39, 59, 97
Open University 80

parents 4, 8, 20, 33, 34, 35–6, 45, 60, 88, 98, 105
passwords 26, 56, 61, 62, 63
PCs 11, 14–15, 32; desktop 3, 13, 34, 37, 39, 91, 98, 102, 105; laptop 11, 42, 98
Pebble Watch 4
pedagogy 22, 39, 74, 93–5, 106; philosophy of 18, 77–8
personas (online/classroom) 75
phishing 64
photos 13, 50, 55, 65, 66, 73, 75, 87, 90
physics 88, 89
plagiarism 28, 72–3
plug and play 13
poetry, writing of 40
police 59
popular culture 57
pop-ups 63
privacy 56–8, 66
Programme for the International Assessment for Adult Competencies (PISA) 22
projectors 41

quality assurance 28
question and answer sessions 75–6, 96

RMstudy 38
Romeo and Juliet 2, 21
Roosevelt, Franklin D. 10
'Ruined Maid, The' 103
runners 49–50

Samsung 32, 105
SatNav 4
schools 11, 73, 77, 78; anti-bullying policy of 57–9; and technology 3–4, 11–12, 105–6
Screwfix 4
SD cards 13
sexting 62
Shakespeare, William 2, 21
short stories 42

Siri 5
Skydrive© 12, 78
slide shows 92, 102
smartphones 3, 4, 5, 11, 12, 14, 19, 31–5, 38, 48, 58, 61, 62, 68, 74, 91–2, 98, 101–2, 105
Snapchat 57, 75
social media/networking 2, 6, 9, 22, 43–9, 53, 58–9, 62, 69, 93; and confusion 47–8; exclusion from 45–6
social norms 57, 59
social services 59
software 3, 11, 15, 34, 37, 39, 48, 61, 64, 72, 75, 77, 88, 89, 96, 97, 98, 106; antivirus 63; firewall 63; picture-warping 57; project management 38; obsolescence of 75; security 63; updating 5–6, 34, 37–8, 48, 63
Sony 13
sound 50, 90, 101
spamming 62, 63, 64
special educational needs 7
spoofing 64
sports 17, 44, 72, 75, 86, 94, 95
spreadsheets 13, 27, 77, 101
streaming 14
students 1, 10, 48–9, 52, 98, 106; art 51; briefing 96; disadvantaged 38, 48; 'pupil premium' 7; hearing-impaired 23; interactive 43–6, 50, 52–3; movement of 99; vision-impaired 7, 23
student safety 9, 33, 34, 36, 47, 50–1, 55–9, 61, 67–8, 78, 106
students' own resources 3, 29, 34
suicidality 56

tablets 2, 5, 11, 12, 14, 31, 33, 34, 35, 37, 41, 44, 48, 49, 61, 74, 89, 91, 95, 98, 105, 106
teachers 1, 7, 9–10, 17–19, 22, 25, 32, 44, 46, 49, 52, 74, 77, 81, 94, 96; contacting 47; English 2, 19, 49, 53, 102–3; geography 44, 45; history 24, 26; ICT; inspirational 1–2, 37, 38; language 91–2; music 89; physical education 2, 6–7, 44, 50, 51, 72; science 27, 88
teaching 1, 2, 3, 5, 9, 10, 15, 17, 18, 22–3, 25, 27–8, 32, 37, 29–41, 43, 44, 47, 50, 51, 52, 69, 75, 77, 79, 80, 82, 86, 93–5, 99, 101, 106; and contextualising 2; inspirational 3, 10, 23; personalising of 2, 41–2
teachthought.com 60
teams, networked 22

technophiles 9–10, 39, 95
technophobes 9–10, 39, 95
television 19
temporary knowledge/skills 6
text messaging 32, 62, 75
3G 14
timetables 17, 106
touch screens 14, 37
travel consultants 14–15
Trojan viruses 60, 64
trolling 62
turnitin© 72
tweeting 38, 50
Twitter 44

United States 60

VDT (virtual desktop) 15
video 2, 28, 41, 44, 49, 50, 55, 73, 75, 77, 87–8, 90, 99, 100; interactive 19; streaming of 14
video lectures 18
viewing rights 28
virtual computing 14–15
virtual learning environment (VLE) 15, 21, 24, 28, 46, 47, 49, 51, 56, 59, 68–9, 72–81, 106; and assessment 76; and good practice 74–5; and opportunities for learning 76
viruses 60, 61, 64

wearable technology 4
web browsers 15, 32, 63
webcams 14
websites 11, 39, 41, 49, 62, 62, 64, 78, 83–4, 87–8
Whatsapp 105
whiteboards 73; interactive 4, 41, 102–3
wi-fi 4, 11, 14, 34, 36, 105
Windows Mobile 11
Windows Moviemaker 92, 97, 99, 102
Windows phones 61
wireless technology 68–9
World War I 100
World War II 24, 25–6, 100
world wide web 15, 58

youth culture 59
YouTube 5, 14, 39, 97

For Product Safety Concerns and Information please contact our EU
representative GPSR@taylorandfrancis.com
Taylor & Francis Verlag GmbH, Kaufingerstraße 24, 80331 München, Germany

www.ingramcontent.com/pod-product-compliance
Lightning Source LLC
Chambersburg PA
CBHW060516300426
44112CB00017B/2692